Review

This writer has a poet's gift for language, a playwright's sense of drama and a stand-up comic's talent for timing. Upon reaching the last page, I found myself turning to the beginning and starting again, not wanting the book to end.

In her memoir, My Sins, A Childhood Memoir of Staying on the Nice Side of God, Voncille Henry takes her readers on a warm, moving, and often comical journey of growing up in an ultra-conservative religious community in rural New Mexico in the 1950s. The memoir is told through a first-person narrative of 10-year-old Vonnie, who has recurring fears of literally "going to hell if I sin once". Ultimately, she finds escape (and salvation) through the piano.

In this format, Ms. Henry is free to observe the girl she once was without the interpretive intrusions that come with age; she can remain true to what she felt then, rather than what she knows now. Her recollections are stark, intimate, and heartwarming. But perhaps most remarkable is the generosity of spirit with which she writes about her relationships with those individuals who impact her life and influence the remarkable and talented woman she became.

Victoria Johnson, M.A.
Licensed Professional Clinical Counselor
First Born ® Founder

My Sins

A Childhood Memoir of Staying on the Nice Side of God

VONCILLE HENRY

A3D Impressions
Tucson | Minneapolis

My Sins:
A Childhood Memoir of Staying on the Nice Side of God

Published by

A3D Impressions

P.O. Box 57415, Tucson, AZ 85735
www.a3dimpressions.com
a3dimpressions@gmail.com

Publisher's Cataloging-in-Publication data available

Paperback ISBN: 978-1-7371922-6-8
eBook ISBN: 978-1-7371922-7-5

Jessica Castillo, cover design
Donn Poll, book design

The stories in this book are true. The names and exact locations have been changed.

Preface

This is a collection of true, tender, and sometimes heartbreaking stories told in the voice of 10-year-old Vonnie, who is growing up on the West Texas and New Mexico border. Vonnie, gripped by Preacher Higgins' fiery sermons about Hell, gives an exquisitely honest account of a child's recurring fears of a literal Hell. Her great love of the piano and the gospel music she hears, in part moderate her terrors, with a little help from the beautiful Janie Larue.

Author's Note

In my twenty plus years as a social worker one thing became very clear, that children are very good observers of adult behavior and of the injustices of life. The faithful entries in my childhood diary prompted this book and a decision to give "Vonnie", aged 10, her voice.

Vonnie's astute observations of life in the 50s and 60s are worthy of report. There are stories in the book, and words from my childhood notebooks that are difficult to read, growing up as I did in a segregated time and place. I knew even at 10, when people were treated as less than, or shamed because of a physical disability or the color of their skin. There were very few people of color in Hobbs, NM, at the time, but the few who lived there kept away and were rarely seen. I knew none, with the exception of a few Hispanic children who attended my grade school.

The language of the church and its exclusivity also triggered young Vonnie's innate sense of right and wrong. Christians giving themselves the right to judge each person's spiritual status as good or bad, saved or unsaved. Women's subordinate roles in the church, even belittlement and disrespect never did set right with my Mother, who was quite vocal in her opinions on the matter. Her sense of fairness for all helped to shine a light on equality and the rights of women for my sister and myself.

I was uncomfortable with what I witnessed and experienced and my young self, Vonnie, felt it all, including the weight of recognizing injustice when others did not. It was the beginning and the formation of a growing instinct to trust myself with my questions. But it was years before I found the courage to ask the questions I needed to ask.

Until my thirties, I left my early religious life locked away. I didn't feel safe examining or questioning the church's teachings. Doubt was considered a spiritual weakness.

The church's specific teachings about Hell had my younger self terrified that I, my family, friends and others that I loved would most certainly end up in Hell if we didn't follow all the rules. All of them.

Going through Vonnie's notebook would reveal not only the pain and misinformation I had, but it would help me reconnect with the insight I had as a child and recognize the resilience I was fortunate to have.

Children hear things they shouldn't and experience things they never asked for. I now have compassion for my young self as I do all children who don't have the language or power to defend themselves. I want to know and honor what Vonnie knew at such a young age and give her a voice. Children will tell us things we've forgotten and probably don't want to hear, but we need to listen. There is healing and wisdom in their words.

Opening Vonnie's diary and being transported by her stories was also a revelation about what cannot be taken away. It became clear how much music anchored me to my sense of self then, and continues to be my anchor today. Music allowed me creativity and joy. Through the piano, I found a way to express myself when other spoken truths would have landed me in a heap of trouble. Playing the piano became my "saving grace", both literally and figuratively, and I hope these stories will help others find theirs as well.

... these words mirror spoken truth
unspoken yet by you

in some mysterious youth
deep in some ephemeral dream
where angels and demons sing

— **Anthony Freeburn, 2020**

Table of Contents

Almost Sixteen

Hobbs, New Mexico   March 1960
15 years old

Preacher Higgins says that one day Moses was up on the mountaintop praying and crying and God said, "Look down there by your foot, Moses." And right there under Moses' robe was a tablet of stone. And sure enough, it was the *10 Commandments* written in cursive.

I have all the Lord's rules to follow, plus my Mom's, and she is extra strict, and then Preacher Higgins'. It is hard to keep up!

What if I can't remember them all? That's why I started keeping a special Notebook of Sins when I was 10 years old. I always took my special notebook to church with me right along with my King James' Bible, and wrote down all the sins I could. It was downright mortifying, and just *no fun*, worrying I might miss a sin or two.

My Mom was extra strict then and now, but since I'm almost 16, at least I'm learning to drive and run errands for her. And I can sit with my boyfriend, Jerry Dean, at church and hold hands if no one is looking, and finally go with the youth group on picnics to Phillips Petroleum Park. But I don't know *anyone* else with so many rules. Well, my Sissy.

If you've ever read the Old Testament, you'll find out it's full of laws and slayings and animal sacrifices and disobedience and thunder and lightning, and if the people behaved themselves, Moses let them have a big feast. They had to work hard and make their animal sacrifices. And in Deuteronomy, God commanded us to remember the Sabbath and keep it holy and that included the slaves and everybody. And I say good for them to get a day off! There's commandments about not lying, or bearing false witness, and loving God even when you've never laid eyes on him.

Some of those 10 Commandments I don't think I have to worry about so much, like committing adultery, or coveting a neighbor's slaves or animals. When the Lord got to the seventh commandment, he was pretty tired, so he rested. After all, he had just finished making the Heavens, the Earth, and the Sea. Whew!

We have to honor our parents and be especially kind, even if they have a million rules. But then we always skip this part: "Make an animal sacrifice on an altar of unhewn stone". I am especially glad we don't do that since I love animals. But how can you just decide to skip over one of the rules? Won't we get in trouble for that? I *think* so!

There's a lot of stuff to scare people in the Bible, especially that scripture in the New Testament about staying ready and sinless all the time—every single minute—for the Second Coming of Christ. Only if I stay ready can I be sure I won't go to Hell, and nobody knows when the "End Time" is, not Preacher Higgins or *even my Mom.*

> *Then two shall be working in the field; the one shall be taken, and the other left. Two women shall be grinding at the mill; the one shall be taken and the other left. Watch therefore: for ye know not what hour your Lord doth come.* — **Matthew 24: 40-42**

I know I sure don't want to be left down here on Earth plowing in a field or grinding at a mill with my Sissy and even though we are so young, all of a sudden, we would be grinding away—and she would go on up to meet Jesus in the sky since she's a good Christian—and I would be left down here with a bunch of other sinners! Preacher Higgins says we'll be punished in the Great Tribulation for seven whole years, and my Mom says things will be so bad people will be fighting over one loaf of bread and killing each other over nothing, and there will be so many bugs we can't put our foot down without stepping on a big pile of them!

I'm still scared sometimes and mixed up at nearly sixteen, but believe me, it was lots worse when I was 10, and that's why I kept my special Notebook of Sins. Last night when I was looking around in my closet, there was my notebook, right next to my King James Bible. I remember trying to stay awake at church, listening to Preacher Higgins' sermons and making that list of sins. I was trying so hard to be ready for the Second Coming and that "Big Meeting in the Sky."

I know this for sure, back then I was afraid all the time that I would forget the rules and do something really bad. When I closed my eyes, sometimes I could see myself in that Lake of Fire with flames creeping up around my shoes and burning my legs, and there was *no one left* to help me!

There I was, only 10, thinking about Hell every day and especially at night before I went to sleep. I'm older now, but I make sure I ask myself every day, "Vonnie, can you be sure you are *saved and right with God?*" I tried when I was five to get saved, but what if it didn't take?
I'm tired of being scared and thinking about Hell, so I don't

know if I should keep that Notebook of Sins or burn it. I'm going to read it again and then decide.

Be Extra Careful at Church

Hobbs, New Mexico   October 1954
10 years old

I found out on accident that kids at church had better keep their heads bowed when the big folks pray, or they may get a thumping! I got thumped on the head by someone that wasn't even my Daddy. But there's a lot more rules than that. I think 75 or 80!

Brother Higgins was preaching on Sunday, and he told the Ladies to listen up, he had something to tell them. He said it is a Sin, a S-I-N, for ladies to wear lipstick and earrings. If they do, they might as well be shaking hands with the devil—all painted up looking like harlots. And just to be ready for the Second Coming of Christ, he says he doesn't want us going to movies or to the Friday night football games.

I don't understand very much of his preaching, so I can always ask my Momma about things when we get home. Except for that word "harlot." I have *begged* Momma to tell me what it means, and she just looks away and says, "You don't need to know".

Brother Higgins, he was preaching and wiping sweat off with his hanky, and crying about the sinners, and after church, my Daddy said, "Poor ol' Brother Higgins. Seems like he cares so much that he worries about Hell all the time".

But I do, too! I'm afraid I will wind up in Hell instead of Heaven, so I'm keeping a list of all the sins I can think of, a special Notebook of Sins, so I won't ever forget them. And since

Brother Higgins says it is a lot easier to go to Hell than to Heaven, I'm trying to change and go "up." I listen *good*, trying to do what our Preacher says even though I'm only 10. I sure don't want to end up in that Lake of Fire with a bunch of other sinners! So, I am writing every day in my spiral Notebook of Sins, and it's extra-extra important because I mostly write about staying out of Hell. And I write about the beautiful Janie Larue, and Sister Annie, and Preacher Higgins, and my Sissy. I write about Janie Larue because of her good piano playing, and I always write about Sister Annie because of her goiter, and I write about Brother Higgins, because of Hell. I write about my Momma, too, because she knows just about everything.

Momma tells me I talk too much, so I'm trying to be more like my Sissy because she is nice and quiet. Before we go anywhere, Momma takes my chin and looks straight in my eyes and says, "Now Vonnie, try not to embarrass me in public". Daddy tells her not to worry, that I am just feisty. That's a word I don't know, but he smiles when he says it, so I don't think he minds how I am.

I wrote my list of sins for me and for anybody else that wants to read it and wants to stay out of Hell.

What *IS* a Sin?

Our preacher, Brother Higgins, tells us plenty about Hell. So, I'm hoping if I stay in church with the Christians at Faith Pentecostal, I might be able to get into Heaven.

I need to learn what all the sins are, even though I'm just a kid, so I am keeping a list, and here are the sins I already know about:

BE QUIET AND BOW YOUR HEAD. I know it's wrong to look around or giggle if people are praying. One night at church I got a hard thump on my head from old Mister Griffin, and when I told Momma, she didn't like it. Now, I'm extra careful.

We pray at home during our family devotions and me and Sissy get down on our knees, and Momma does, and Daddy does. We have to be quiet and Momma tells us to pray but I don't know what to say to God way up in the sky, so I kneel down extra low so I can look at my Momma's face upside down.

DO NOT TAKE THE LORD'S NAME IN VAIN. I know it is a sin to cuss, but I wouldn't do that anyway. I'm not even allowed to say gosh or golly, because Momma thinks I might slip and say "God" on accident.

DO NOT FIGHT. I know Sissy and me are not supposed to argue or fight, but I don't know if that's really a bad sin, or if Momma and Daddy just don't like the fussing and hollering. It would be hard for us to quit since Sissy is so mean to me.

DO NOT TELL LIES. I know it is a sin to tell a lie and I don't need to lie because our house is so little and crowded, Momma sees everything me and Sissy do. There isn't any way to sneak around or fool her. My Momma is like God.

Sissy told me it's a sin to touch ourself, "down there." She said it is so bad that people can't talk about it. So, I said, "OK, smarty pants, if people can't talk about it how did you find out?" Sissy said, well, she thought she read it in the Bible. But sometimes Sissy is no fun, so I think she made it up. I can touch myself if I want to. Sissy wants me to add it to my list of sins, but I didn't.

DO NOT WEAR LIPSTICK OR EARRINGS. It is a sin for grown up ladies to wear lipstick and earrings. Only one person gets by with that, and she is old and has what Momma calls a big goiter that she covers up with a pretty hanky. Sometimes, I take my little cousin, Nannie, over to look since I've seen it over a hundred times.

The ladies at church are allowed to wear necklaces and beads, and I am glad, because that means I can, too! For my school picture I put on my double string pearl necklace I got for Christmas and I wore my Dutch girl barrettes in my hair so I would look extra good.

GROWN UP LADIES SHOULD NOT CUT THEIR HAIR. The ladies at our church can't cut their hair because of what St. Paul said about it. Momma says there's a scripture in Corinthians where he says women are "dishonored and sinful" if they cut their hair. Besides that, he says that women should "always cover their heads before the Lord".

My Momma won't do it. She won't cover her head, and she tried once to let her hair get long, but it was thin and stringy, so she told my Daddy, St. Paul can think what he wants to about it, but she was going to cut her hair and get it curled!

Since St. Paul doesn't tell men to grow their hair long, too, my Momma gets good and mad, and she says it just isn't fair, because everyone should be treated the same.

I keep hearing about more sins to add to my list. But the next part I wrote down is really important because I want to learn how to stay on the nice side of God.

One Sunday at church Janie Larue played a song about going to Heaven called *I've Got a Mansion Just Over the Hilltop*. When she played, I thought about Janie and how beautiful and special she is. Janie Larue is already 16 and everybody knows she is a perfect Christian. And because Janie can play for church, I think it will probably keep her out of Hell. If it does, I wonder if I could learn to play at church, too, because I would do anything to stay out of Hell!

I am still learning about more sins that can get me in trouble but maybe I can be just like the beautiful Janie Larue, and not feel so scared about Hell all the time.

Summer Revivals and Women Preachers

We knew a revival meeting was coming to Faith Pentecostal in the summertime, but when Brother Higgins told us the preacher's name was Winona Rae Sparks, a woman, *and* a preacher, *and* a piano player, lots of people didn't like it. But, boy I did!

Momma says some people just don't like the idea of a "woman in the pulpit", and some of them, even the ladies think women have no business trying to take a man's place in church.

But this preacher lady looked different. She wasn't skinny or wearing pretty high heels like the other evangelist ladies. She was big and as tall as my Daddy. After he saw her, he said, "I believe she could 'whup' me in a minute; but I sure do like her mean, ragtime piano playing." I didn't know what ragtime was. I just knew I loved hearing it, too, and after that I decided to learn how to play ragtime my own self.

I like revival meetings and going to church every night because there is always a lot of special music. It is way better than staying home and playing dolls with Sissy. And sometimes the revival preachers bring their wives along wearing their fancy clothes. Once a preacher came with his whole family and every one of their four kids played a musical instrument. I was little then, but Momma let me sit right on the front seat because I didn't want to miss a single note. "I want to be a musician, too, Momma," I told her even though back then I was just seven years old.

The singing is always good at Faith Pentecostal. We clap our hands and some people get up and do a little jig if they feel happy. Momma's friend, Sister Billie Lee, plays her tambourine. I love the sound it makes when she slaps the tambourine and makes the little bells jingle. Brother Tilley brings his fiddle. If he is tired, he won't even stand up. He just plays sitting down on the front seat. He puts the end of the fiddle on his chest and closes his eyes when he plays. He is real old.

But a lot of people didn't like our revival preacher, Sister Winona. They said men are supposed to be the preachers and they aren't *ever* going to change their minds! So, some people, mostly the men, stayed home and waited out the revival. But Momma thinks it is just fine for women to preach. She says women are just as good as men and smarter a lot of the time. My Momma usually picks sides with women.

Some people don't like my Momma because she will tell the truth and say how she feels about things even if it makes somebody mad. And she doesn't mind telling my Daddy what she thinks about most everything. She is downright mad about some of the things in the Bible. She says women have as much sense as men and usually *more*, so she doesn't agree when St. Paul says men are supposed to be the "head of the house".

Sitting at the breakfast table one morning with Daddy, she shook her head and said, "It just doesn't make sense. Old Brother Tucker can barely find his way home from church, and his wife, Ginny, went to Business college and supports the family. *She* should be the head of the house!"

So, Momma asked Daddy, "How does the Bible explain that? You tell *me*!"

Momma was good and mad, and getting pretty loud, so, Daddy

said, "Aw, Hon, don't take things so hard." But Daddy didn't know what to tell her, either.

During that same summer we had another revival and this time the evangelist was not just one, but two women! They are sisters and they both have hair the color of a pumpkin! Their names are Viola and Marla Dudley. But after a few nights, Viola came to the revival all by herself. She stood up and apologized and said her sister, Marla, left to go get married so they couldn't finish the revival. But everybody loved Viola except for her preaching, so Sister Higgins found a job for her, helping out with Sunday school for a while.

Going to church every night is okay with me and I am always able to stay awake through the special music. But mostly the preacher wants lots of people to get saved and filled with the Holy Ghost. So, there's always a long alter call begging the sinners to come down and get saved before it's too late. Church goes on and on!

When it comes time for the sermon and before the preacher starts reading out of the Bible, I get a few songbooks and stack them up for my pillow. I pull my feet up under me and lay my head down on the books. I try to fall asleep even when Brother Higgins is preaching loud and scaring us about Hell and that Lake of Fire.

Maybe I ought to stay awake and listen, but I get too tired. And I always keep thinking about Hell like the grownups want me to. I keep on making my list of sins to be sure I won't end up in that big, fiery lake. And while I'm lying there, I think about Janie Larue and how special she is to God because she plays the piano at church and doesn't wear lipstick or go to movies and dances. I *know* she won't have to go to Hell. Maybe that's why Sister Winona and the Dudley sisters decided to preach. They thought preaching would keep them out of Hell, too. Maybe Momma wants to stay out of Hell, and that's why she keeps going to church even when she is mad at St. Paul.

I close my eyes under the bright lights, feeling so tired. I remember when I was little, my Daddy would pick me up and carry me out after church and lay me down in the car, but now I'm too big. Sometimes when I'm falling asleep, and I feel like I just can't stay awake any longer, it's all right because I can hear two nice preacher ladies with bright colored hair, singing me to sleep.

Our Brand New Piano

When I was eight, Daddy found me and Sissy a nice piano for only $50. He said since we didn't have much money, that was just exactly the right price. That night, before Daddy went to pick it up, I was way too excited to sleep. I knew by tomorrow, I would be looking across the bedroom at our new piano, and it would be the first thing I would see every day! Momma said, "it has to go right *there*," across from our bed, because there wasn't any other place in the house for it. I begged to stay home from school the next day and wait for the piano, but Momma said absolutely not.

Daddy bought the piano from Skippy's Momma at church and she said somebody gave it to her 20 years ago. The next afternoon Daddy closed his garage early to go load it up and I could hardly catch my breath I was so excited. I was afraid it might not really happen. But if it did, by suppertime me and Sissy would have a piano sitting right in our bedroom!

After school every time a car went by, I ran to the screen door to see if it was Daddy's pickup. Finally, Daddy drove up and I could hardly believe it, but right there was our new but old piano, so heavy, it made the back of Daddy's truck slant down. I ran outside to watch. Daddy had brought three men to help, and it took them so long just talking and planning how to get my piano down out of the truck, I got scared.

Daddy looked things over, shaking his head and talking to the men. I could feel tears coming behind my eyes, but I blinked them back. Daddy finally went to get his heavy-duty car jack out of the his garage behind our house and set it up. They pushed the piano out of the truck real slow, and once they set it on the jack, one man on each corner, Daddy lowered the jack, and they set the piano all the way down on the ground. It was so big and heavy, they carried it three or four steps, then they had to stop and put it down so they could rest a minute. I was so worried I went racing back and forth from the house to the truck. When they finally got it to the back door, the piano was too wide and they moved it this way and that. It still wouldn't fit, so after talking and planning, they took off the screen door. They kept trying and it still wouldn't fit, so then they decided to take out the wooden door. I was ready to pop just watching them! Daddy finally said, "Vonnie, you need to step out of the way." But I wanted to see everything that happened. By the way they were all grunting and sweating, I was scared they were going to drop my piano. And if I am going to learn to play at church like Janie Larue, I *need a piano for practicing*!

I could tell by looking at my Daddy's face he was getting so tired. If they couldn't get the piano through the door, I knew they would have to give up and then take it back to Skippy's house. Tears were burning my eyes, but I kept my fingers crossed behind my back to help them out. After Daddy counted to three, they lifted the piano up and barely squeezed it through the door. It started to lean from one side to the other, and my Uncle Mack hollered, "Watch out!" They waited until they got it straight up again and set it down on the floor, and *finally* pushed it up right next to the wall! Daddy and his helpers got out their hankies and wiped the sweat off their faces, and then plopped down on the bed to catch their breath. My Uncle Mack strained his back so bad he was bent sideways the next day. But *finally*, our piano was ready to play, with a piano bench in front, and me and Sissy, we got busy playing it! All evening, and the next day, too.

It was the biggest, tallest piano I had ever seen and it was a funny color, but I didn't mind at all. It looked like somebody took a giant brush and painted it brown. Momma laughed and said it was exactly the color of poo, but to me, it looked perfect because I wanted a piano more than *anything* and having a piano right across from my bed was way better than Christmas! But the best part, our piano would be there every morning the first thing I could see when I opened my eyes. None of the pedals worked but I didn't care. That day and the next I played way past our bedtime.

Sometimes when we are in town, Momma will stop and wait for a few minutes so I can go inside and play a few of the new pianos at Curley's Music Store. And the people there don't even mind that I'm just a kid, so I go in and play any new piano I want to.

But our big, old, *brand-new piano* is the best one of all.

Backsliding and Cigarette Smoking

Aunt Mindy and Nannie ride to church with us on Sundays, but Uncle Mack stays home and smokes his cigarettes. Nannie always climbs in the car and squeezes over next to me wearing her Sunday dress and holding her little plastic purse. Nannie is only five. Aunt Mindy and Uncle Mack live so close that we can walk to their house, and Sissy and me play with Nannie while our Mommas drink their coffee. Aunt Mindy is an extra good Christian because she is so nice and kind. And she especially loves children. She is my very best Auntie!

Last time they were having their coffee, I don't think I was supposed to listen, but I heard Aunt Mindy tell Momma that my Uncle Mack has bad stomach trouble, and that's why he can't work. Aunt Mindy said things are so hard she guessed she will have to get a job herself. So, my Auntie got a job making pies and sandwiches at the soda fountain at Woolworth's.

Aunt Mindy was busy making her pies and sandwiches in the daytime and when she came home, she had all the cooking and dishwashing to do since my Uncle Mack was sick. After a while, my Auntie's hands got red spots and sores on them and when she showed them to Momma, she looked at Aunt Mindy's hands under the kitchen light so she could see better. "Why Mindy, I think that strong dish soap you use at the soda fountain is causing this." Aunt Mindy looked down at her sore hands, "Millie Faye, I have got to keep working. All I can think to do, I guess, is get me some rubber gloves. I can't quit now." She was worried and I was, too.

I felt sorry for my Aunt Mindy not knowing what to do about her poor hands. She *had* to wash all those dishes. So sure enough, she got herself some big, yellow gloves to use in her dishwater. The sores didn't go away, but she had to keep on working.

And then one afternoon after work she and Nanny came over, and what a big surprise she gave Sissy and me! Aunt Mindy sat down at the kitchen table and she opened up her purse and took out a cigarette! I went straight over to ask her about it, but Momma gave me a big frown and shook her head no, so I went back and sat down. I had never seen my Auntie smoke, and only my Uncle Mack smokes, out of all the people I know in the world, except for my best friend, Connie, but her Momma doesn't know.

I was watching everything Aunt Mindy did. She leaned her head over and put the cigarette in her mouth, just holding it between her teeth while she struck a match. I would have helped her, and I especially like striking matches, but I didn't offer because of Momma.

Momma probably wanted us kids to go on and play, but I wanted to know all about this smoking my Aunt Mindy did. She told Momma she started smoking because she is feeling so jittery and nervous about everything, and when she's trying to relax, she thinks it helps her. She said, "I know smoking is bad and I know what Preacher Higgins will say, but I'm worried to death and scared about money and then there's Mack with his problems. But just because I'm smoking doesn't mean I'm backsliding." Aunt Mindy stopped for a minute. I watched her close, and she mashed out her cigarette in the saucer Momma gave her, since we don't have ashtrays. Aunt Mindy looked worried. "Well, maybe it is true. When I think about it, I've been so busy working and taking care of Nannie and Mack, I've missed a lot of church, and now here I am smoking these cigarettes. Maybe I really am backsliding!" She looked scared.

I didn't know what Aunt Mindy meant. When they left, I said, "Momma, what is backsliding?" She told me and Sissy, "Backsliding is when people forget the Lord, turn their backs on him and slide right back into sin." It scared me to think my Aunt Mindy might be backsliding and going to Hell because of her nerves, when she was just trying to smoke and relax.

The next Sunday, they didn't ride to church with us, but when I looked around, Uncle Mack must have brought them because Aunt Mindy was sitting at the back of the church, and Nannie came, too. I was glad my Auntie was there, just in case smoking *is* a bad sin.

Some churches don't do it, but at our church, we always have an altar call after Brother Higgins' sermon, even if it's just Wednesday night Bible study. Brother Higgins says he won't *ever* close a church service without warning sinners to turn their life around and get saved and filled with the Holy Ghost.

Today, while Brother Higgins preached, he took his hanky out of his pocket. He unfolded it and wiped up the sweat on his face. He always preaches hard and loud. The Invitation comes after the preaching, that's the altar call when sinners can come up to the front to get saved and maybe get the Holy Ghost, too. My friend, Ruby has the Holy Ghost and she is just 11. I haven't got it yet, and that's another thing I'm supposed to be trying to get, but Momma says I can wait a little longer. I don't think I like praying and having to speak in tongues, but that's what you have to do. But now the altar call is coming, and Brother Higgins likes for Janie Larue to sit close so she will be ready to play the piano.

I especially don't like this part of church when our preacher cries and hollers and explains about Hell. It scares me to death, and I don't know what a kid like me is supposed to do. I think I'm saved, but then maybe when I was five and I was praying and hoping to get saved, maybe it didn't work. I don't know how to find out, either!

But Brother Higgins, he says the Invitation is the *most important* part of church when sinners have a chance to make the biggest decision of their whole lives, so I *have* to listen to him. Janie always plays the piano with the soft pedal on while Brother Higgins talks. Today she is playing the song *There Is A Fountain Filled with Blood*. I know all the words…
> …*drawn from Emanuel's veins,*
> *and sinners plunged beneath that flood,*
> *lose all their guilty stains.*

Ooh. I never like touching blood.

While Janie plays, Brother Higgins, with his face all shiny, stops to take a swig from his water glass. Today, I think he is especially worried about the sinners, because he is preaching about sin and evil and how it looks, "tempting and fun"; and how quick and easy sin can slip up on us. Now he's taking off his coat and laying it down on a bench. His voice is getting loud again and pretty soon he starts hollering and waving his arms, then all of a sudden, Brother Higgins *throws* his hanky down! And he looks mad! "AND, I've got something to say to the backsliders: If you aren't ON FIRE for the Lord and living a good, clean life, then *you* of all people need to come back to God! It's downright serious when we get too comfortable, taking things for granted with the Lord! God *hates lazy*, lukewarm Christians! In fact, in

Revelations He says, 'Because you are neither hot nor cold, I will *spew thee out of my mouth*!'"

He was preaching loud, and it seemed like he was too worried to stay put, so he came down from the pulpit so we could see and hear him even better; and I think he was getting scared none of the sinners were going to get saved so he preached louder and louder. He preached, not hardly stopping for a breath, and he finally said to the sinners, "It is *dangerous* for you to wait another minute to come to God!"

It takes a lot of energy for Brother Higgins to preach and holler such a long time and he usually gets so hot he has to take his coat off. But today even with his coat off, being so worried about Hell and everything and his face all red, he especially needs his hanky to wipe his face and neck. He reached down to pick it up again. I could see he was getting real tired, and Janie Larue kept right on playing with a serious look on her face. I had a serious look on my face, too, because when he preaches it scares me!

"Now, Folks, I'm begging you, give up your selfish pride, come just like you are, full of sin and shame, kneel down at this altar and there won't be a need to suffer in Hell. It's as simple as that," he said.

Poor Brother Higgins was crying, just thinking about everything. He took the Bible in one hand and pointed to it begging us to think carefully, and he said, "This is God's word, not mine!" He wiped the tears off his cheeks and told Janie Larue to play *Just as I Am* while we sang. "Folks, we are going to wait while you make this important decision." Then he folded his arms and closed his eyes and waited.

When I looked over, I saw my Aunt Mindy walking past us. She was bawling and heading to the front. She almost fell on the altar, her head down and her tears making little puddles. Everyone kept singing, but then the ladies came and knelt beside her and put their arms around her. Everybody prayed loud, asking for Jesus to wash her sins away. I wasn't sure my Auntie was doing anything wrong and whether she needed to get saved all over again. But I sure don't want her to go to Hell either!

Then Nannie came running over to Sissy and me. She was crying and looking so scared. I guess since she is little, she didn't understand what her Momma was doing and if she was all right up there, crying and praying. But I'm already 10, and I have seen people trying to get saved before. So, Nannie climbed up on the pew and I pulled her over close to sit between me and Sissy. I whispered in her little ear, "Nanny, don't be scared; your Momma is just getting saved again and don't worry." So, Nannie stopped crying and sat there with us while we waited for her Momma to finish getting saved.

Finally, the noise and the praying slowed down and Aunt Mindy stood up and wiped her eyes, looking for Nannie. Nannie got down and ran and hugged her Momma and everyone came back to their seats. Brother Higgins finished the service with a prayer and said he sure was thankful Aunt Mindy came back to the Lord!

I think that means she will have to quit her smoking. Brother Higgins told everyone to come back tonight for Sunday night services. "And remember, God doesn't like slackers."

On the way out after church was over Momma told Aunt

Mindy, "Don't bother with cooking today. Let's go get Mack and we'll have Sunday dinner together." So, Momma finished the roast beef and vegetables and put them on a plate while me and Sissy set the table and poured the iced tea. Everybody got around the table to eat just the way I like it: my Aunt Mindy, Uncle Mack, Little Nannie, my Momma and Daddy, and Sissy. Exactly the way it's supposed to be.

I just love it when they come over to eat with us. But today I like thinking that now since Aunt Mindy is saved again maybe people can stop worrying about her going to Hell. But even more than that, I want to stop worrying about going to Hell myself!

Doublemint Gum and My Momma

On Wednesday night when church is about ready to start, I go ask Momma for some chewing gum. She always gives Sissy and me gum, if she has it and usually she does. If she runs low, sometimes we have to split a half-of-a-half of a stick of Doublemint gum, and that's not very much! Momma always wants to be fair, so I watch her break a stick in half and she is real careful to tear the silver paper just right, and I get a half and so does Sissy.

When Momma opens up her purse, I take a nice, minty smell of Doublemint gum. Her purse is off limits to everybody, even my Daddy, but sometimes I can unsnap it for her and take a nice, deep breath. I like to snap it back and forth a few times, but then Momma always grabs it and says, "Vonnie, you're gonna wear that out!" After I got my gum waiting for church, Momma looked me straight in the eye and said, "Now, don't be smacking your gum."

Since I am 10 years old, Momma says I can sit on the front seat at church as long as I behave myself. It's all because I want to watch Janie Larue, the most beautiful girl in the world play the piano.

When Janie sits down at the piano, she spreads her skirt all around her and she stretches out her foot with her spike-heel shoe and she puts it right next to the pedal. She sits up really straight and folds her hands in her lap and waits for church to start. And Janie Larue always smells so good!

Another reason I like to sit on the front seat is because once

Brother Higgins starts preaching—and that's my most unfavorite part of church—I can turn around and watch Sister Annie sitting behind me. But sometimes, sitting back at her seat, my Momma sees me staring at Sister Annie, and she makes a circle with her finger and that means I have to turn around.

Sister Annie is one of my special friends and I can't stop looking at her. She has a big goiter on her neck, and she uses a pretty hanky to cover it up. And not just the goiter, she is the only lady at Faith Pentecostal Church to get by with wearing earrings and lipstick.

But not everyone likes Sister Annie as much as I do. Some ladies don't like her because of her lipstick and earrings, but that is some of the reason I like her! Some of the grownups, they don't like her because she has a son who is a "Negro". But I will always keep writing about Sister Annie, because she's the only person I know anywhere with a goiter.

My Momma likes church but since she always sticks up for women, she told Daddy there are lots of things in the Bible she won't agree with. Momma said, "Why is it OK for a man to just up and decide he wants to divorce his wife and put her out on the street? That's what they did, and it says so in the Old Testament. All he had to do was to say three times, 'I Divorce Thee, I Divorce Thee, I Divorce Thee'!"

That didn't sound right to me either. On top of that Momma is plenty mad at St. Paul since he decided men were going to be the head of the house.

"Some men are too dumb to be in charge of anything," she told Daddy, "and I'll name them if you want."

"Oh, no, that's OK, Millie Faye."

Momma knows my Daddy is smart, because he has his own auto shop business. I don't know if that makes him the head of our house, but if you ask my Momma, I think she would say no.

But there's someone my Momma especially hates. And that is my Daddy's mean step-dad Mister Tom. And he's dead, but me and Sissy knew him, and he bossed my Grandma and he sat in his big easy chair all day claiming he was a preacher and quoting the Bible. He told everybody he was "God's messenger", but my Momma didn't believe it. "Why, he's just an old reprobate," Momma said. I wasn't sure what that meant but it sounded bad.

My Momma doesn't like him because Mister Tom told my Grandma and my uncles everything to do and not do. And Momma is extra mad because he made his own wife call him "Mister Tom", but Momma is the *most* mad because he said he is a "Prophet of Jehovah."

"Prophet, my foot!" Momma said. "He's got no business treating his family the way he does. Everybody, I mean *everybody*, I don't care who they think they are, they've got to treat their wife and kids right!" she said.

My Daddy agrees with her. But if Daddy bosses my Momma, she will jerk her head around and look at him with mean eyes and say, "OK, Bill. Let's see how far that kind of talk gets you." When Momma is mad, she calls my Daddy, "Bill." All the rest of the time, he is "Hon."

My Momma says if it's ok to have men preachers it's just fine to have lady preachers, just like Sister Winona, the big lady preacher that plays honky-tonk piano; or Sister Viola, with the bright colored hair, or her sister Marla, but Marla left in the middle of the revival to go get married.

My Momma wants everything to be fair, just like the Doublemint gum. She always breaks it slow and even for Sissy and me, so nobody gets cheated.

But I think I know why Momma wants everything to be fair. When she was growing up she had an older brother and Momma says he tormented her day and night, thinking of mean things to do. When I looked up "torment", the dictionary said, "To afflict great bodily or mental suffering on someone." One time, when she was four years old, her brother did the meanest thing I can think of. He pulled my Momma's mouth open and made her taste of… yes, poop! She cried and screamed, but he laughed and said she'd better keep it to herself or something worse would happen.

So, Momma didn't tell. Her Mother, my Grandma Pierce, is big and fat with extra fat arms and hands. She has short, grey hair and glasses. When she looks down at me through her glasses, her eyes are big, scary circles. She wears flowery dresses and fluffy house slippers. Grandma P. talks loud and bosses my Grandpa and all the little kids. I told Sissy, she is *not* my favorite Grandma.

My Momma says she and Grandma P. never did get along. Grandma used to tell my Momma she was "fat and ugly, and never would amount to anything." So, I think that's why Momma can't believe how pretty she is and instead she thinks she is ugly! Momma likes for things to be fair, but in her family, they weren't.

But my Momma is wrong thinking she is ugly. My Daddy, the handsomest man in our church picked Momma because she is pretty and smart, and everybody thinks so. But if my Momma remembers what a bad time she had when she was little with her mean brother, and how wrong it is her own Momma said she was ugly, then I hope my Momma will start feeling pretty, since she is but she doesn't know it.

Preacher Davis and the Lea County Jail

Back when I was six years old I went with Momma and Daddy and Sissy to the Lea County Jail. Only six or seven prisoners decided to come to the jail service. Maybe they didn't care about God or Jesus, but they just wanted to take a look at my Momma, looking extra pretty in her Sunday dress and her high heels, wearing her little gold cross my Daddy gave her. Sissy and me wore our twin dresses and Daddy and our preacher, Brother Davis, were still wearing their Sunday suits. We stood there while they looked us over. Pretty soon Momma would be singing for the prisoners and Brother Davis would be preaching. He doesn't have a church, so he asked the jail people if he could preach there, and they were glad to have him. Brother Davis will probably get a real church, because now he is rich.

No one knew this would happen, but one day just like that, Brother Davis struck oil. Daddy drove us by to look and right there next to his house I saw a big, black machine pumping up and down and making a loud racket. Momma and Daddy laughed and joked when they were talking about it. I didn't know why, but then I didn't know what striking oil meant, so Daddy told me and Sissy that now Brother Davis is rich. Daddy said, "Even when he didn't have a dime to his name, Brother Davis gave money to everybody that needed it, so he deserves to get rich!"

Brother Davis is a real good preacher, so he took some of his striking oil money and bought the vacant lot across the street from us hoping he can build a real church of his own someday. But since he doesn't want to wait, he preaches to the prisoners on Sundays. He can do the preaching, but since he wanted it to be just like church, he asked my Momma and Daddy to do the singing. They are extra good singers, so on Sunday after we went to our real church, Brother Davis used to come by to pick us up in his Cadillac. He bought his brand new Cadillac with some more of his striking oil money because he had so much of it. Sissy and me got to ride in the front seat and Momma and Daddy sat in the back, holding hands.

Since we were getting ready to have a church service, the big folks decided to pray all the way to Lovington. They prayed about everything. They prayed for the prisoners that fell into sin and ended up in jail, they asked Jesus to save them and fill them with the Holy Ghost, they prayed for the Lord to protect us while we were driving to the jail, they prayed for me and Sissy to be good and be a light on the paths of others, and they prayed for the unsaved wherever they are, hoping they will get a better life. It was twenty miles from Hobbs and a long time for Sissy and me to be still and be quiet. And back then, I was *only* six years old. I didn't like the car trip but it wasn't all because of the praying.

Brother Davis is nice and an extra good Christian, but I didn't like it when he drove the car with his eyes closed. I guess he believes the Lord will always keep us safe no matter what we do. He only peeked out from his praying just long enough to keep the car on the road. But I didn't take my eyes off him all the way there. Cars zoomed by us when his eyes were closed, and he was looking up just once in a while, still praying for everybody! Since me and Sissy aren't supposed to interrupt the grownups when they pray, I didn't know what to do. Once, the car headed over to the dirt and Brother Davis jerked it back. Sometimes, from the back seat my Daddy would yell, "Watch out, Brother Davis!" Sissy and me were so glad when we finally got there!

Brother Davis parked his car and we walked up to the Courthouse. The Lea County jail has four stories. The best part of all, though, is the elevator! It is the only one we have in the county, Daddy said. But I bet it is the best elevator in the whole United States!

Me and Sissy ran ahead of the grownups to be first on the elevator. Mr. Gunn, the jail owner, smiled at us and opened the elevator doors. I think he knew that what we were going to do is real important to the Lord and Jesus.

But the jail owner, Mr. Gunn, was taller than any man I ever saw! I looked all the way up to the top of his head. He wore brown clothes with a shiny badge on his pocket and I counted 13 keys fastened to his belt. When we stepped inside, he pushed the elevator button and the big doors closed and down we went! When we landed with a bump, me and Sissy grinned at each other.

The elevator opened and we walked over to two big, metal doors. Mr. Gunn unlocked them and when they opened, I smelled pine cleaner like Momma uses when she mops our floors. I think it must take a lot of scrubbing to keep a jail clean! Mr. Gunn walked over to where there was a whole row of iron bars. When I asked what they were for, Momma whispered, "Vonnie, the bars are there to keep the prisoners from running away. And since they broke the law they have to stay in jail."

We waited behind for the jail owner. His keys clinked until he found the right one, and he bent down and unlocked the iron bars to go get the prisoners. I couldn't wait to see what a prisoner looks like! Pretty soon they came in and lined up against the back wall, just looking us over, especially my Momma. I like it when Momma wears her church dress with the silver belt. Me and Sissy, we wore our best Sunday dresses and they were just alike. Momma says it feels to her like she has twins, and it's easier to dress us alike.

There were seven prisoners. Some of them leaned against the wall with their arms crossed looking mad. They were mad because they had to stay in jail and they knew we could get out. They all looked nice and clean in their khakis and I'm pretty sure Mr. Gunn told them they had to get cleaned up for Jesus. He came back out and locked the iron bars behind him and stood off to the side so Brother Davis could do his preaching and we could do our singing.

Brother Davis walked up to the bars and started the jail service by saying he was glad the men had decided to come and hear the word-a-God and said he would start off with a prayer. He prayed for the prisoners, and their wives and children waiting at home, then he asked Daddy to lead a song. Daddy sang out in a loud voice, *Friendship with Jesus*. I was only six, but I knew every word of church songs, so me and Sissy sang loud right along with the big folks. Sometimes one of the prisoners sang a little if he knew the words. Some of them went to church I decided, until they got caught.

Next, Brother Davis asked Momma if she would sing a solo. I could tell Momma was a little bit nervous. She cleared her throat and put her head back and sang. My Momma sings loud! She says she doesn't know how to sing quiet. I always listen and that day she sang one of my favorites, *Mother's Bible*. The ladies at Faith Pentecostal like it special, and when she sings it, they cry and wipe their eyes with their hankies. But the prisoners watched close without taking their eyes off Momma.

*In my hand I hold a treasure, oh, I praise it beyond
measure,
for it brings to me such memories of old;
With its pages worn and wrinkled, spotted where the tears
were sprinkled, Mother read it by the fireside long ago*

*Tis my Mother's dear ol' Bible,
Dear ol' precious worn out Bible...*

When she finished singing, I saw one of the men wiping his eyes. And I know why! He was thinking of the trouble he was causing his own dear old mother!

Brother Davis preached for a while then he stopped and asked Momma and Daddy to sing, while he invited the prisoners to come forward to surrender their lives to God and make a new start. Momma and Daddy were singing *Softly and Tenderly Jesus is Calling*. After a little while, one of the men did come up to the iron bars and Brother Davis talked quiet to him, almost whispering. I think he was probably trying to figure out what to do to stay out of jail. But Hell is lots worse than jail and I'm trying to stay out of Hell anyway I can!

Brother Davis reached through the bars and put his hand on the prisoner's shoulder and then they knelt down and prayed. After the prisoner was saved real good, they stood up. Since he got saved with all his sins washed away, Brother Davis asked him to "say it out loud and let everybody know that you have accepted Jesus as your Savior." So, the prisoner turned and looking down at his feet in a shaky voice he said that he accepted Jesus and wanted to do better. Brother Davis reached through the bars and shook hands with him, and he turned back and went to stand with the other prisoners.

When our church service was over Mr. Gunn unlocked the iron gate one last time. He locked it behind him and took the prisoners back inside. When he came out it was time for us to go home. But me and Sissy, we were excited to get one more ride on the elevator!

We got in Brother Davis's fancy car for the trip back. I watched Brother Davis all the way, hoping the grownups were all done praying so he could watch the road better, and they were. And, they got their prayers answered because one of the prisoners got saved!

Sometimes in the morning, we open our front door and we can hear Brother Davis across the street praying. He prays so much I think he's got "saint's knees." My friend, Sister Annie, says she has saint's knees too, but my Momma doesn't believe her.

But Brother Davis never wrecked his car because of his praying or we would have read about it the next day in the *Hobbs Daily News-Sun*.

Momma and the IRS

I thought maybe having me and Sissy for her kids was the best thing that ever happened to my Momma, but she didn't say anything about us. Instead, she said the two best things she ever did in her life was to get saved at the country church when she was 18, and marry my Daddy, William J. Clark.

My Momma is so smart that when she was in High School they gave her the name "vale-dic-tor-ian." I had to look up the spelling. She said her Momma and Daddy were so poor with seven kids, she couldn't even get enough money together to go to college over in the next county. And that was "all I ever wanted to do," she said.

My Momma didn't get along with Grandma Pierce, so she decided to leave home and take a job in town, working for a rich lawyer family in Lubbock, cooking and cleaning.

When Momma had the day off, she went back to her house out in the country to see her friends. One Sunday, Luella and my Momma went to a Gospel Singing at the church. There sat my Daddy, so handsome with his black wavy hair and his big smile. He spotted my Momma with her red hair—she had just Henna dyed it, she told me and Sissy. Daddy asked Momma and Luella if they wanted to take a ride in his Ford coupe. It turned out my Daddy liked Momma so much he picked her up for a date the next week. "That was just how it was supposed to go," Momma says, and they got married a year later.

That same day Momma went up to get saved at the little church. She said she felt good afterward, and she felt like things were going to turn out all right. She said she was looking for a way to feel happier, and maybe church was just the right thing.

So, I think Momma is glad to keep going to church with Daddy and taking me and Sissy to Faith Pentecostal Church even though she gets mad about men being the head of the house. Momma says the only thing we can do about our troubles is pray to God and hope everything will turn out all right. She prays when she is worried and scared about things, and so does my Daddy.

Daddy doesn't talk much about it, but he had a real mean stepfather growing up. Momma says, "When I hear about the things that old man did, and how your Daddy grew up, I'm amazed your Daddy is so happy, and so kind to everybody." He will fix people's cars for free, if they are broke, just like he helped old Miss Mabel. His mean stepdaddy, Mister Tom, believed he was a specially good Christian, and he even preached part-time. He said he heard things "straight from the Lord," but Momma says he used church and religion as an excuse to treat people awful, especially his wife and kids. Momma says it just isn't right. "Why, he's a plain old hypocrite," she told my Daddy, and my Daddy didn't even argue with her!

Momma can't stand hypocrites and I think that's why she won't make friends with Sister Annie at church. Momma thinks she is a hypocrite. But I sure am glad she lets me be friends with her. Sister Annie always wears her lipstick, even when she's not supposed to. I always check to see when I go up to look at her goiter before church. I look at her goiter, and I look at her lipstick. I like Sister Annie and I think about her goiter a lot, and I will keep writing about my special friend.

One day, when I went to get the mail for Momma. I handed

her a long, brown envelope and after she opened it, my Momma looked like she had seen a ghost! "Oh, Lord," she said. I couldn't even guess what would scare her so bad. She picked up the envelope and ran over to Daddy's garage to show him. Finally, after I *begged* to know what it was, Momma said, "Well, Vonnie, it's a notice from the government. Whether we want them to or not, they are coming right here to our house to make sure we aren't stealing their money." Momma said the IRS found a mistake in her bookkeeping, and she would have to get out all her records from my Daddy's shop. "… and knowing what 'thugs' they are, they will try to make us pay a lot more money!" My Momma was plenty mad, but looking at her face she was scared, too. I could tell. Daddy went over and put his arms around her and said, "Well, Hon, I think it's going to be alright."

We went back home, and Momma walked straight to the closet and got her box down where she keeps her papers for Daddy's shop. She put the box with the records on a shelf so she could grab it in a hurry, when they came for her. She shook her head and said she guessed there wasn't anything she could do but keep her records out ready for those IRS people and just pray. She worried the whole day and I could see it was a good time for me and Sissy to play outside.

After that, during our devotions when Momma read from the Bible and then we got on our knees to pray, Momma reminded the Lord that she needed help. She told the Lord, "I'm just like poor little David in the Bible! I am up against the mighty Goliath, the IRS!" After a while I forgot all about the scary letter from the tax people, and even Momma stopped talking about it.

One day for lunch Momma made fried chicken with mashed potatoes and gravy. She had set her hot rolls out that morning to rise, and for dessert she baked Daddy's favorite, coconut cream pie. Momma is a real good cook. My Daddy is a picky eater but he loves his coconut pie. Thank goodness, she still makes lots of chocolate cakes for me and Sissy.

We were getting around the table ready to sit down when a man with a big satchel knocked on the screen door. Daddy went to the door, and when the man said he was Mr. Wilson, from the IRS, Momma's face turned white. He told Daddy he needed to look at Momma's records. Momma just sat staring for a minute.

Daddy said, "Well, come on in now, Mr. Wilson. Have you eaten your lunch yet?" They were looking down at the table full of good food Momma cooked. "We were just getting ready to eat and you're welcome to sit down and have some lunch with us." My Momma and Daddy always invite people to eat if they stop by.

Mr. Wilson looked down at the fried chicken and taters, and off to the side was the coconut pie. After a minute he said, "I believe I will." So, Momma fixed an extra plate for him. It was crowded at the table so me and Sissy took our plates to our room to eat. When we all finished eating, Momma cleared the table and set the dirty dishes in the sink. She went straight to the shelf and got out her books for the tax man to look at. By then, Mr. Wilson had his coat off and his tie, and seemed real glad to be sitting there talking with my Daddy about the hot weather.

Sissy and me peeked around the corner watching to see how Momma and Mr. Wilson were doing. He scribbled on a pad, and kept looking back at Momma's records, working away at the kitchen table, checking on her arithmetic. Momma sounded scared but she answered all of his questions. After a while he took another drink of iced tea, scooted his chair back, and pulled the strap over to fasten his satchel. Then he stood up. He looked at my Momma and shook her hand and said, "Mrs. Clark, you did a fine job with your bookkeeping, and the mistake was the governments, not yours." She smiled the biggest I *ever* saw, and that smile stretched across her whole face!

Mr. Wilson took his satchel and left with his belly full of chicken and coconut cream pie, to help him remember my Momma's good cooking and her extra good arithmetic.

Our Cousin Gracie and her Momma Pansy

Uncle Howie's trailer was so teeny that Momma said she would probably need to do the cooking for him and my cousin, Gracie. "Why, that kitchen is not much bigger than a matchbox," she told Daddy. Not only that, Uncle Howie doesn't know much about doing laundry either, and since he has a kid to take care of, Momma said she would do that for them, too.

When I found out that Uncle Howie and Gracie were going to move their trailer right in next to our house, I jumped up and down and hollered, I was so excited! Gracie would be living right in our back yard! Sissy and me could play with her every single day and show her the way to school and play games up in the attic. And besides that, we are just like stairsteps: Sissy is oldest, Gracie is in the middle and I am the youngest.

Gracie has big, brown eyes, and sometimes they look sad, and she gets quiet and won't play with us anymore. Momma says that is when she is missing her Momma and "pining" for her. Her Momma left Gracie and her Daddy a long time ago.

When Gracie was a baby, Aunt Pansy, went off one day and Uncle Howie didn't know where she was. He couldn't find her anywhere and Momma said Gracie was still a baby then, and she cried and cried for her Momma. Then Gracie's Momma came back and stayed a while and left again.

But, now, me and Sissy have someone we can walk to school with! I like walking down the alley by the Chuck House Cafe. I can look inside and see the people sitting in the booths eating their breakfast. The waitresses wear white dresses and white shoes. We can smell the bacon and biscuits cooking. Since the booths have windows next to the street, I especially like looking in and thinking about the people from California, staying at the motel across the street from Daddy's garage, and now they are eating their breakfast and getting ready to go back to Hollywood. I know I will be eating at the Chuck House for breakfast when I'm all grown up. And someday I plan to live in California, too, probably in Hollywood.

We always walk by the gas station going to school, and the Elm Tree trailer park. Next, we tiptoe around the trash and tumbleweeds where the fancy La Miradora Hotel used to be. We can look down in the dirty swimming pool full of old bicycles and broken toys and trash, since they had to close the hotel. Sissy met up with her friend, Arlene, and they walked on ahead of us. Gracie and me walked together.

We had just stepped up on the sidewalk at school by the front entrance when a lady came over with a big smile on her face.

"Hello girls," she said in a friendly voice. We just stood there. She came over closer. "Don't you know how to greet your Mother?" she said, smiling at Gracie.

Then Gracie cried out, "Momma!" She had seen her Momma's picture. "Momma! What are you doing here?"

"Well, I wanted to see my girl." Then Aunt Pansy came close and reached down to give Gracie a hug and kiss. We didn't know what to do next. I don't even know her Momma, Aunt Pansy.

Then Aunt Pansy smiled, looking at Gracie, and said, "Well Sweetie, I haven't seen you in such a long time, would you like to go for a Coke?" By now, Gracie couldn't stop smiling and looking back at her Momma. I guess she was getting excited, thinking that her Momma has finally come home!

"OK, Momma, I'll go with you!" So, they left with Gracie holding her Momma's hand, and I went on to school.

But something seemed funny to me, and I thought I should go call my Momma. Mr. Drew, our Principal was right there at the front door greeting the kids, like he does every morning. I tapped him on the arm, so he bent down. It was real noisy and hard to hear, so he had me come into his office. Then I told him about Gracie's Momma showing up and what just happened. I asked him if I could call my Momma. He said, "Sure, of course, Vonnie, that's a good thing to do."

When I called my Momma she got real excited and she seemed scared, talking louder and louder. She said she was afraid that Aunt Pansy wasn't telling the truth about "going for a Coke," and she might not bring Gracie back to her Daddy. I hung up the phone. Later on, I found out that Momma ran next door to tell Uncle Howie, where he was helping my Daddy at his garage, so he went straight to the telephone and called the police! The police asked him a lot of questions that he couldn't answer, like what kind of car they drove and what was the license number and from what state. He didn't know any of the answers. By now, though, the police figured that Aunt Pansy had taken Gracie past the Texas State Line, only five miles away. The police said it's just too bad that they can't do anything once the car leaves the state of New Mexico and especially since Gracie was with her real Momma.

But all day at school, I went on thinking that Aunt Pansy was a nice lady and would bring Gracie back right after their coke.

When school was finally over, me and Sissy ran all the way home to find out if Gracie came back home to her Daddy. Maybe her Momma would stay, and that would make Uncle Howie happy, too. I opened the screen door, and Momma was sitting in a chair twisting a handkerchief first one way then another. She looked like she had been crying. She said, "Well, girls, Gracie is gone. It looks like Pansy took her away and probably won't bring her back."

Nobody talked at supper that night and no one felt like eating the food Momma cooked. Later on, me and Sissy cried ourselves to sleep.

The next day everything was strange. Gracie didn't come in with her Daddy for breakfast, or brush her teeth in our bathroom. Sissy and me walked to school without her, just hoping her Momma, Pansy, would bring her back. Instead of playing kick ball at lunch like I do every day, I sat on a swing all by myself just thinking how I missed my cousin and how much she would miss Sissy and me, her Uncle Bill and Aunt Millie Faye, but more than anybody, her poor Daddy.

That was three years ago, and we still don't know where she is. But, I still cry sometimes for my sweet cousin, Gracie.

Sunday Dinner and Brother Stone

We have soul-saving revivals at Faith Pentecostal. I didn't know what that meant, so when I asked Momma, she said that means we are "bringing sinners to the Lord and saving souls right there at Faith Pentecostal church in Hobbs, New Mexico. It doesn't matter who they are. Everybody, rich and poor, they need to be saved and filled with the Holy Ghost." She said to make real sure everybody hears about Jesus, our church has missionaries they send to faraway places. And Momma said that just like our church in Hobbs, they are trying to get souls saved all over the world, too.

Brother Stone is a preacher and a friend of my Momma and Daddy. When he comes back from preaching in El Salvador, he stays at our house. I like that because I just *love* having company, and Brother Stone, he teases and laughs with Sissy and me. He is what Momma calls a missionary. She said he is to go with us to church and try to raise money so he can go back and preach to the sinners again.

Sunday morning, I woke up with my hair tangled in the legs of the kitchen chair. Sissy and me gave Brother Stone our bed, so Momma put down blankets for us in the kitchen. I felt something cold on my cheek when I woke up and I had rolled off my pillow onto the floor. When I scooted back on, I remembered it was Sunday morning and we had company at our house! Momma made one of her Milk Chocolate Cakes last night for our Sunday dinner. Chocolate is my favorite of everything, and Momma makes cakes so often, she says she could probably make one with a hanky tied over her eyes.

I love having company stay overnight at our house. Sissy and me always sleep on the kitchen floor with blankets for a mattress. Brother Stone apologized to us for taking our bed, but I didn't care at all. In fact, I wouldn't mind sleeping on the kitchen floor every night just so we could visit and talk with the grownups. I get so loud and excited that Momma shushes me and says to be quiet so the big folks can talk.

Since our cousin Gracie's Momma snatched her away, her Daddy, my Uncle Howie, lives all alone in his little trailer. So now, since Gracie is gone, Brother Stone might start staying with my Uncle Howie, but I hope not. When he goes from village to village preaching, Brother Stone says he might sleep on the bare ground, so any bed at all feels nice to him.

Next morning at church I sat right on the front seat because I wanted to see everything that happened. Janie Larue, our piano player, was off on a trip but it was all right because Brother Stone brought his guitar and played for us. When he started talking, sometimes he caught himself speaking Spanish not even planning to! He played and sang some of the songs he learned in El Salvador for us. He even taught us a Spanish song *Hay Poder*.

> *Hay poder, Hay poder, Hay poder*
> *En la Sangre de Jesús, Hay poder*

I didn't know what it meant but I learned it anyway. We sang and clapped our hands and before you knew it everybody could speak Spanish!

Brother Stone brought a slide projector with him and pictures of his church in El Salvador. He came down the middle aisle and turned it on. The motor made a loud racket but he said he was used to preaching loud so everyone could hear. I saw a picture of a white building for a church, not much bigger than a garage. But sometimes, he said he preaches outside when he travels from place to place. Brother Stone said most of the people there have never seen an American or seen a beat-up Ford truck. They walk from miles away and some ride donkeys, he said, just to hear about the word-a-God.

I always wanted to see pictures of a foreign country and all those unsaved people. But instead we saw people having their parties and festivals. I can't believe people live in such a pretty place where there are dark, green hills and mountains. It's not like Hobbs, with sand and tumbleweeds! The girls and their Mommas wear skirts with yellow, green, red and purple colors, and their white blouses are embroidered with puffy sleeves. The women tie their babies on their backs and just keep working outside.

After church, Momma was in a rush to leave since she was cooking Sunday dinner for Brother Stone, Uncle Howie, Daddy, and me and Sissy. She had been getting things ready since last night when she stirred up the dough for her hot rolls. She said she would roll them out before church so they would rise up big and puffy when she baked them. Sissy helped her peel potatoes so Momma could mash them. Then she got the chicken frying. At the back of the stove, she was frying up okra and squash dipped in cornmeal. I was hungry so I was watching everything she did.

Momma says our kitchen is too little for even one cook so me and Sissy took the hint and got out. Momma had steaming pots cooking on all four burners, and boy, was it hot in there! At just the right minute, she will put the rolls in the oven to bake.

So, the rest of us waited and waited. Me and Sissy gave up and did some coloring. I was so hungry it seemed like it took Momma five or six hours at least to get things cooked just the way she wanted them. But Sissy said, "No, it couldn't be that long, or it would already be suppertime." Brother Stone and Uncle Howie waited on the red couch. Daddy sat in the big chair, all of us waiting. After a while, Momma sneaked a roll to us, "… just so you won't faint", she whispered to Sissy.

Finally, after what seemed like a whole long day passing by, the food was ready. Momma called us to the table. Our table is jammed against the wall with just barely enough room to get four chairs around it. Momma had put her best tablecloth on, the one with roses and vines. She gave Brother Stone the chair at the head of the table and when we got settled, Daddy asked him to say grace. Sissy sat at the corner by Uncle Howie on a tall wastebasket turned upside down. I sat on a stool and left a chair for Momma.

"Eat all you want," Momma said, once Brother Stone finished saying grace. She got busy serving food and filling our glasses with iced tea. Momma's fried chicken matched the color of our honey jar up in the cabinet. Boy, did it look good. I couldn't wait another minute, so I took a big bite from a chicken leg. I love the salty taste of fried chicken. In the middle of the table was the mashed potatoes and gravy and my favorite vegetables, crunchy fried squash and okra. Momma sliced some tomatoes, and we had hot rolls and butter. I knew there was dessert, with a chocolate cake Momma had baked last night. She let me lick the big spoon, covered with cake batter and Sissy scraped the bowl, and I still don't know who got the most. Probably Sissy, because she always does!

We filled up our plates, all but Momma, and she walked past us and went over to the red sofa. She laid down and pulled her feet up and closed her eyes. Daddy kept calling her to eat, but she said, "No, thanks. I'll enjoy it more after while." Later on, she said she had worked so hard in a hot kitchen for so long, all she wanted was to lay down and put her feet up. So, that's what she did. She said she knew it was her only chance, since there would be a "truckload" of dishes to clean up once everybody finished eating.

Momma didn't stay on the couch long because she wanted to serve the dessert herself. After we ate breakfast this morning, I watched her make what she calls "Seven Minute Frosting." She mixes the sugar and egg whites and then she beats it for seven minutes! When the frosting was finally ready, Momma had it standing on that cake in peaks, like little white Christmas trees! I was thinking about that cake all morning during church and Sunday school.

Momma always gives Sissy and me a giant, grown-up size piece of cake. She says she likes to see her girls eat all they want, because when she was growing up, she was so poor she didn't have quite enough to eat. I loaded a big bite of cake on my fork and let the sweet chocolate melt on my tongue. I ate all of it slow to make it last. I was hoping to have some leftover after Sissy finished, but it was so good, I ate every bit of it and even scraped the plate before Sissy finished. Then I had to just sit and watch Sissy eat all of hers. She didn't offer to give me any, either.

Uncle Howie had to loosen his belt he had eaten so much. After the men left the kitchen, they took their chairs out to sit in the shade and Momma got started with the dishes. She had her water boiling in the teakettle and she used her big soup pot for rinsing. She filled the sink with hot water and soap and started washing. First the plates and glasses then the silverware, pots and pans. She stood Sissy and me over by the kitchen table and gave us clean tea towels, so we did the drying. By the time we were done the table was loaded and stacked with clean dishes end to end.

Finally, when everything was clean, my Momma filled her plate with fried chicken and all the vegetables and went straight to the red sofa. She ate her Sunday dinner with her feet up and a pillow tucked behind her back. She set her glass of iced tea down on the end table.

Watching her eat and grinning at her, I said, "Momma, I just love Sundays." She gave me a little wink.

Momma rested in the afternoon and we ate the rest of the fried chicken for supper, and it was cold right out of the icebox. Because Momma, she said she'd done all the cooking she planned to do for a while.

Miss Harper and the Christmas Display

Miss Harper, our music teacher at Hobbs Elementary, is *old*. I don't know how old, but I think she might be about ready to die. She is grumpy and cranky and once when my friend Connie asked her how old she is, Miss Harper said in a snooty voice, "Don't ask grown women how old they are, Connie, it's not polite." But then another time before class Miss Harper said we could guess her age if we wanted to. I said, "Miss Harper, I think you are 70, 80, or 90." She stared at me for a long time and then she said, "I am 45 years old, thank you, Vonnie."

Miss Harper is strict, and I am scared of her just like everyone else is. She sends a lot of kids to the Principal, so after she looked at me with a mean look, I shut up and took out my songbook *American Songs and their History*. I like to sing, and I am a real good piano player, but it is just no fun having music with Miss Harper. She makes us sing from a songbook nobody ever heard of. Today we sang *The Yellow Maize of the Plains* and *The Lope of the Antelope*. None of the fourth graders can read music except for the smart ones like me and Mary Lou. Miss Harper can't play the piano as good as me, in fact she has to bang out the melody with one finger and with only two of us being good musicians, me and Mary Lou sing loud for her.

But Miss Harper is usually nice to Sissy and me and I think I know why. Number one, she needs me for my good singing and music ability, and number two because my Daddy fixes her car for her. My Daddy is always nice and fair to everyone that comes to his auto shop, so I think that she needs my Daddy's help, and my help.

Before Christmas, Miss Harper said she needed help with the

snow scene in the display case in the main hall. And she called me over and my best friend in the world, Connie. I love getting out of class, so Connie coming along was extra nice.

Miss Harper borrowed two step stools from the library for us to stand on. She pulled the curtain back in the display case and right there before my eyes was a pretty, winter scene with mountains, tiny pine trees and cotton for snow, with a little pretend lake made with a mirror. There were tiny ski people that she put on top of the hills. Miss Harper had made the hills and mountains by using wadded up newspaper, and then she covered it all up with soft layers of cotton. The skaters on the pretend lake were dressed in scarves and hats, skating and smiling. I had never seen anything like it.

Miss Harper said, "Now, Vonnie and Connie, listen carefully. I just need your help picking up the stray pine needles from the cotton, and nothing else. I'll come back soon to check on you. Remember, that's all I need."

She left, and me and Connie grinned at each other and started zooming the little skater people around the pretend lake back and forth. Then we helped the ski people go higher and higher on and off the hills. Pretty soon they went higher and higher out of the case, over Connie's head and mine. We played and giggled, almost forgetting we were still in school, so Connie shushed me to be quiet. I thought I heard Miss Harper coming and we hadn't even started our job, so we got busy and lined up all the skaters and skiers in a row at the end of the display case. We didn't quite know what to do next, so we folded up the cotton. Next, we took the wadded-up newspaper that made the little hills and were just finished piling it up in the corner when Miss Harper came back to see if we were finished.

We were finished all right! Miss Harper looked like she had seen a ghost! And then, I remembered what it was she had told us to do, *Pick up all the little pieces of pine needles. Don't do anything else!*

I got really scared watching her face. Her eyes bugged out and her mouth turned sideways, and she said, "What on earth were you *thinking*, Vonnie? And you, Connie?" Her voice got louder and louder and she was almost screaming at us, "Were either of you listening?!" Then Mr. Drew our principal, and Mr. Bigley, the Superintendent, came walking past. Miss Harper gave them a funny smile. When they turned the corner, she said in a low, croaky voice, "Just look at what you've done! This will have to be done all over again!" We all three stared at the mess we had made.

"Well, Miss Harper," I said, hoping she would smile, "We can help you fix it back." She looked at me with hate in her eyes. "You get your little *be-hind* back to class, Vonnie," she said, "and you too, Connie." Her hands were making fists, so I hurried and jumped off the stool and went back to class.

That night I told Momma all about it and told her how mad I was at Miss Harper for the way she acted, and for yelling at me and Connie, but Momma was cooking supper and she didn't even look up when she said, "Vonnie, you have *got* to learn to follow directions!"

Miss Harper didn't put the winter scene back up and the display case sat there with the big mess that me and Connie made. After a while, I just turned my head the other way so I wouldn't have to look. But I was real careful in music class after that and sang nice and loud to please Miss Harper, and I made real sure I behaved myself.

The Short Music Lesson

It was Saturday and I was glad. After our chores are done and our hair is washed and curled, Sissy and me always walk four blocks to downtown. We love going to Woolworth's where my Aunt Mindy works at the soda fountain, making her pies and sandwiches. Right across the store, my friend Annie works at the candy and nut counter.

Last Saturday, when no one was looking, Annie filled the big metal spoon full and running over with M & Ms and dumped them in my sack. She handed it to me and said, "That'll be 25 cents, Vonnie." And I know Annie was just being silly, because they probably cost at least a dollar. But I wanted those M & Ms, so I took them anyway, paid her my quarter and said, "Thank you, Ma'am!" But we had to get to our piano lessons at Mrs. Hays' house, so Sissy said we could stop by Woolworth's on our way back. We walked past Jackson Drugstore and right past Woolworth's. After our piano lesson, I was planning to climb up on the stool at the fountain and order myself a Cherry Coke. Ordering a Coke from my Aunt Mindy makes me feel all grown up even though I am a kid.

First thing I did was plop down in Mrs. Hays porch swing. At home, we don't have a porch swing. We don't even have a nice porch, so while Sissy had her lesson I decided to sit outside and swing until Mrs. Hays called me for my turn. Sissy opened the door and Janey Tucker stumbled out with her music books in her arms and her face looking really mad. Maybe Mrs. Hays was bossy to her like she sometimes is to Sissy and me.

Mrs. Hays mostly teaches the violin, but not many people in Hobbs want violin lessons, so she teaches piano lessons to help pay the bills. She and her husband, Shorty Hays, moved to Hobbs from Chicago, Illinois. I am pretty sure Mrs. Hays liked living in a nice town in a beautiful house, and now she is stuck in Hobbs. Uncle Howie thinks Hobbs is the stinkiest town he's ever been to. There aren't many trees, and when the wind and sand are blowing, a kid like me can barely stand up to walk.

That day, Sissy started the piano lesson off with her scales. Then she started her chord inversions. It was getting cold and the wind was rattling the window next to the porch swing. So, I went inside. I headed to the bathroom down the hall and Mr. Shorty Hays waved at me from the bedroom. He was sitting in a chair with his leg propped up on a footstool.

I know Mr. Hays because he works at Bower's Grocery store. Mr. Hays jokes with Sissy and me and says funny things when he sacks our groceries. Mrs. Hays told Sissy and me last week that he had injured his foot and was staying home for a while.

I used the bathroom and washed and dried my hands. Before I left, I tiptoed so I could get a look at myself in the mirror. I turned off the light and went back down the hall. When I passed, Mr. Hays called and said, "Vonnie, come take a look at my pore, old foot all bandaged up." So, I went to take a look. "I've been hobbling around on one foot for two weeks and now I'm stuck here with nothing to do." Then he said, "It gets really quiet and lonely in here, all by myself. You're such a sweet little girl, Vonnie. Come over here and let me give you a hug." So, I went closer. "I'm so glad you came in to see me," he said.

Mr. Hays was wearing striped pajamas. All of a sudden, he took me and set me on his lap. I don't even know him that well. Then he put his arms around me and squeezed me hard. "See how hard you can squeeze me," he said. So, I did, I tried to squeeze as hard as he did, since kids are supposed to do what the grownups say. Mr. Hays laughed and told me he had always liked me in a special way. I was surprised because we just see him once in a while at the grocery store. Then he started moving me around on his lap back and forth. I couldn't understand why he liked, even loved me so much all of a sudden. He kept talking and scooting me across his pajamas, and shaking himself up and down. I tried to straighten up and jump off his lap, but he laughed and squeezed me and said, "Oh, no you don't!"

I didn't know what he was doing but I wanted him to stop. I told him, "I want to go." He held me even tighter. Finally, after the shaking stopped, he did let me go. I pulled away and went toward the door. "Vonnie," he said, grinning at me, "be sure to come back and see me again next week."

But I didn't like what he was doing to me one bit! I was mad that he wouldn't let me go. And I didn't know what he was trying to do! I felt all funny inside. I wanted to go home right then, but it was time for my piano lesson. When I sat down at the piano, I told Mrs. Hays I didn't feel well, so I only did one scale, then she cut my lesson short. I got my music books and Sissy waited on the porch for me. On our way back, I told Sissy what that Shorty Hays did. When I told her that it made me feel funny and bad inside, she decided we were going to go straight home to tell Momma. We walked past Woolworth's and went right home not stopping for anything.

When we got home, Momma was cooking lunch. "Momma", Sissy said, "Vonnie has got something important to tell you." So, I told Momma that Mr. Hays pulled me onto his lap, and kept me there when I tried to get up. That he was shaking himself, and it felt funny and wrong to me. And when I told him I wanted to get up, he didn't let me. Momma looked worried. She took me over to the table and we sat down. I told her more about what happened. Momma listened, then she put her arm around me and said he was downright *wrong* to do that, and I was smart to try to get up and leave! With her arm around me I felt a little better because even though I couldn't explain things very well, it seemed like Momma understood that I didn't want him to do what he did, and it wasn't my fault.

After a while Momma looked at me and said, "Vonnie, honey, would you like to take a nice, warm bubble bath? I'll put some of my gardenia bath salts in for you and some dish soap to make bubbles." So, I tore off my dirty, old clothes and climbed over the side of the bathtub. I lowered myself all the way down into the warm water, my feet touching the end. I laid my head back, and all I could see were foamy, white bubbles. I closed my eyes and the smell of Momma's gardenias filled my nose.

I wasn't sure what happened with that old Shorty Hays, but I wasn't NEVER going near him again!

Old Miss Mabel and the Paper Boy

When Sissy and me finished our Cheerios and Daddy went next door to his garage, Momma said, "Well, girls, we need to go help Miss Mabel out a little bit. Get your shoes on and get ready to go to the store for me." We went over to Miss Mabel's trailer park to visit her once before. We didn't know Miss Mabel from church, like everyone else. I'm not sure Miss Mabel is even a Christian because she doesn't go to church and she smokes her cigarettes. But my Daddy knows Miss Mabel because he gave her a free battery and got her old, rusty pickup running and Miss Mabel never forgot what he did. Daddy said Miss Mabel is sick and can't even leave her trailer for food or anything so Momma said she would go look in on her.

Momma cooked up a pot of chicken soup, and while that was cooking, she sent Sissy and me over to Miss Ellis's grocery to get some eggs, milk, and bread. She said if the bacon is on sale to get that, too.

When the soup had cooled off a little bit, Momma poured it into two big jars. We got the sack of groceries and drove over to Miss Mabel's house. I had been to her trailer once before, and I sure do like going there because everything is so teeny! Momma stepped up on the little porch and knocked and called out, "Miss Mabel?" From inside we heard a croaky voice say, "Come on in, the door is unlocked." I opened the door since Momma was carrying her purse over her arm and a jar of soup in each hand. Sissy was carrying the groceries. There she was. Miss Mabel was sitting in front of the window at the end of her trailer house with an orange, crocheted blanket on her lap, like my Auntie makes. Her feet stuck out the bottom and I could see her white, crackly legs. She was wearing some fuzzy brown slippers. Miss Mabel put out her cigarette when we came inside and it's a *good thing*, because her trailer was so cloudy with smoke I could hardly breathe! I could tell Miss Mabel was happy to see us, and her voice got stronger and she said, "Oh, Mrs. Clark, do come in! I was hoping someone would stop by. I've been so sick with bronchitis." Then she took a bad coughing spell and gagged and spit in a red bandana. Miss Mabel was pretty sick!

Momma sat at the end of the little sofa and put the soup jars and her purse on the floor. We set the groceries in the little kitchen. Me and Sissy found a wood chair in the corner and after she caught her breath Miss Mabel said, "Oh, Honey, just put those books on the floor." So, we emptied the chair and sat close together watching Miss Mabel. She was wearing a pink robe with coffee stains down the front. Miss Mabel has long, yellow fingernails, and her white hair has streaks of yellow in it. Even her teeth are yellow! Her skin looks rough and crinkly. I'm pretty sure she is 90 years old. Maybe she is 100!

Momma waited until she finished another coughing spell, then she said, "Miss Mabel, I'm so sorry you've been sick. Has your son been able to check on you?" Miss Mabel wiped her mouth again and shook her head. "No, he's been working in the oil field and hasn't had time." Miss Mabel took a drink of water. My Momma talked to her like she was a good friend, but we don't hardly know her. Momma listened while Miss Mabel told her about how she landed in Hobbs, so she could get to lower elevation and get some fresh air for her bad lungs.

I looked around at the trailer and to me it seemed like a make-believe house. Behind the little toy kitchen, you could see Miss Mabel's bed piled with blankets and clothes. She has a teeny stove with two burners, and next to that is a sink not much bigger than a sheet of notebook paper!

Me and Sissy just sat and watched because we never met anybody like Miss Mabel with her yellow teeth and fingernails and her smoky house. But when I thought about it, I decided living in a tiny trailer could be fun, and I would think about getting one for myself when I'm able to get the money together. But I would put up lacy curtains in my trailer and I would open the windows for some fresh air. And I don't think I would smoke.

Momma asked Miss Mabel if she would like us to heat her up some chicken soup. Miss Mabel clapped her hands and said, "Oh, would you do that?" Momma found a pan and poured the chicken soup in to heat. She put the milk in the little icebox down under the counter, and the bread and eggs on top.

While the soup was cooking, I went over and sat down on the little sofa and I asked her, "Miss Mabel, have you always lived in a trailer?" She said, "No, but this is all I can afford." I told Miss Mabel I thought it was just fine and a good place to live. I told her that when I'm older, I plan to look into buying one for myself. Miss Mabel said, "Well, Vonnie, when you do find your trailer, I hope it is a real nice one."

Momma finished heating the soup and carried the bowl over to Miss Mabel with a hot pad. Beside the sofa where Miss Mabel sat was a footstool, so Momma put the soup there with a spoon in it. Momma asked her, "Miss Mabel, when you're feeling better, would you like a ride to church some Sunday morning?" Miss Mabel thought for a minute and said, "Thank you, Mrs. Clark, but I really never go to church." That seemed fine with

Momma even though she wants everybody to be a Christian. Maybe Miss Mabel is saved after all and isn't even worried about going to Hell. If she doesn't worry, I wish I could be like Miss Mabel.

Momma picked up her purse and said it was time for us to go, and she hopes Miss Mabel will start feeling a lot better. Momma said she would come by again in a few days to check on her. Miss Mabel smiled a big smile and said she didn't know what in the world she would have done today without the food and the nice visit. I went over and shook Miss Mabel's hand and I said, "Miss Mabel, I hope you feel better real soon." Miss Mabel pulled me over to hug me, I could smell the cigarette smoke in her clothes and hair, since my face was right against her pink robe.

We drove home, me still thinking about Miss Mabel and her smoky house, and when we got home we saw Virgil, the newspaper boy, standing and knocking at our front door.

"Oh, dear," Momma said. "I hope we can catch him before he leaves." So, she stopped the car real quick, and rolled down her window and called him. Virgil is our paper boy, but he is not a boy. Momma says he is 35 years old.

Sissy is a little bit afraid of Virgil because he is so big and he weaves around when he walks, like he could fall any direction. Momma told us that while Virgil was being born something happened to him at birth that affects his balance and that's why he walks so funny. I am pretty sure Virgil likes his job of selling papers and he does a real good job of it. He carries a big leather bag full of newspapers across his shoulder. But he is so tall and rickety! Me and Sissy always move back out of his way because he is so wobbly and shaky when he tries to walk. Momma talks to him like everything is normal and just fine, but when he tries to answer her, he wrinkles up his face, and takes a big breath and his words come out loud and choppy. Momma gives him all the time he needs and just waits for him to finish. I don't understand any of his words, but my Momma does!

When they were finished talking, Momma handed him a check for $3.50. Virgil's hands don't work very well together because of shaking, but we waited while he opened his book and handed us a receipt already written down for him. He gave Momma today's copy of the *Hobbs Daily News-Sun* and turned around to leave. He rocked on his feet and it looked like he might fall backward, but then he got his balance and went toward the door. Momma thanked him and said to tell his folks "hello." He stopped and took a big breath and said, "Good-bye!"

Virgil has been our paperboy for as long as I can remember, and I like it when he comes over.

The Chocolate Milkshake and Miss Vonnie

Preacher Higgins wants a new church and I do too! Every Sunday the water goes higher and higher in the toilet in the Ladies' bathroom almost spilling over the edge, and it scares me nearly to death! I run out the door yelling for help!

So, the grownups cooked up a plan on how we could build a new church without costing a lot of money. No one at Faith Pentecostal has very much, so they decided we would have to build it ourselves. Well, our Daddies would have to, and everybody else would have to do their part. The kids in our Sunday School have saved money for as long as I can remember bringing nickels and dimes and putting them in a red bucket. Preacher Higgins is always sending around a special offering plate for the building fund. We need a new church right now!

The ladies decided they could help, too, by cooking supper at home and making some extra food to share. They had the idea that if the men came straight from work, everybody could eat at church, then they could go back and work until they got too tired to keep going. Momma cooked her food, and we helped her carry her covered dishes to the car and then she tucked a big towel around them to keep them warm. We left for church every night as soon as Daddy finished at the shop. The men worked a little while then everybody stopped to eat. After they finished eating, they went straight back to work, and the ladies cleaned up.

I just loved it because every single night, the kids got to play all evening. The grownups didn't even watch us, and we played hide and seek all over the neighborhood and in the parking lot. The church was almost ready for the new roof. One night we were playing tag in the parking lot when a little blue car pulled up in the street and a lady rolled down her window and hollered, "Hey Kids, is there going to be a church meeting tonight?" Some of us went straight over to talk to her, except for Sissy. I'm not bashful like my Sissy. I told the lady, "No Ma'am, there's no church tonight, the men are trying to finish up our new church." They pulled their little car over, and her husband turned off the motor. I guess they just wanted to get better acquainted. The other kids went off to play again, but I stayed. Momma says I'll talk to just anybody!

The lady looked at me and smiled and she said, "You're such a cute girl. What's your name?" I told her my name is "Vonnie." "What? What did you say???" She got really excited, "That's my name, too! Joe, me and this little girl have the same name!" She giggled about our names, then Joe, her husband, peeked around her and said, "Well, howdy do, Vonnie! Nice to make your acquaintance." I was just as surprised as she was!

Miss Vonnie showed me her little dog, whining and wiggling. He was so cute and fuzzy. I love dogs and we don't have one, so I reached in and let the puppy lick my fingers. Miss Vonnie said, "Oh look, he likes you!" Then she looked at me and said, "Listen, Vonnie, Joe wants to go up here to the Dairy Queen for ice cream. We won't be gone long, and I'll let you hold the puppy. Why don't you come along, too. Does that sound good?" She said they would get ice cream and come right back.

I liked this new lady, and she was saying nice things about how pretty I am, and I especially like it when someone tells me so. "I love going to the Dairy Queen," I told her. I looked around to tell Sissy I was going with them, but I didn't see her, and the lady said they were coming straight back. "OK, I'll go, too!"

She opened her door and leaned her seat forward so I could hop in the back. She handed me their cute little dog over the back of her seat. "Here, you can hold him. His name is Teddy." He was so wriggly, but I liked riding around in their little car holding their dog. He licked my face and chewed on my ear!

We went toward town and right to the Dairy Queen. Mr. Joe asked me, "All right, Vonnie, what is your favorite ice cream? You get to pick." Momma and Daddy just buy us cones, so I said, "I would like a chocolate milkshake, please." So, Miss Vonnie got one, too, and boy was it good! I didn't even have to share with Sissy. I told Miss Vonnie, "I sure do like your little car!" I made sure to thank Mr. Joe for the ice cream.

We left and Mr. Joe put some music on the radio. We didn't go back the way I thought we would. Maybe we were taking the long way home. The dog fell asleep in my lap. I was thinking I might be in trouble because I forgot to ask my Momma if I could go with Joe and Vonnie, so I said, "Miss Vonnie, I think I need to go back to the church, now, please." "Oh Sweetie, are you getting tired?" "No, but my Momma is probably looking for me and I forgot to tell her I was going for ice cream." "Did you hear her, Joe? She's getting worried that she didn't tell her Momma. Let's take her back."

My ice cream wasn't tasting so good anymore. I knew Momma would be really mad at me for going off with strangers, but they were so nice. Finally, he stopped and turned the car around. I knew I might get into big trouble with Momma, but I would just have to be brave.

We got to the church and Miss Vonnie opened her car door and I said, "Thank you," and got out. They drove away. Sissy and Momma were out in the parking lot looking for me, and they were really worried. Momma had a funny look on her face. She looked scared and mad all at the same time. Sissy whispered, "You are in a lot of trouble, Vonnie." Momma didn't say anything, we just went inside.

Well, I didn't get punished for going off with strangers for ice cream, but Momma and Daddy both scolded me good. I promised them I won't get in the car with strangers ever again, even for a chocolate milkshake, and I told them I would be extra careful.

Aunt Mindy (front) and Momma

Vonnie with Daddy and Momma

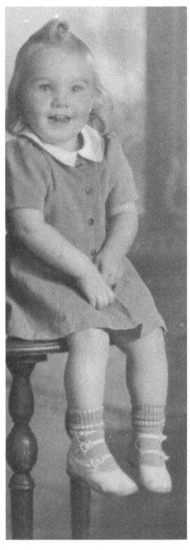

Momma, Daddy, Vonnie, right

Vonnie

Vonnie, age 8

Vonnie, 10

Momma

Vonnie in center

Cousin Gracie and Vonnie

Daddy's (left) shop

Vonnie (18) with baby

Masters Degree Graduation

The Tent Revival

I like sleeping late in the summertime, but one morning I heard hammering and yelling and when I looked out the screen door, I saw people putting up a giant-sized tent. Since Preacher Davis struck oil and gets paid a whole lot of money, he bought the vacant lot across the street. He preaches, but he doesn't have a church, yet.

I yelled for Sissy and Momma to come look, and we saw Brother Davis's new Cadillac parked right next to the pickup trucks and the tent raising up behind them. I couldn't wait to go over there to see what they were doing. I hurried to finish my corn flakes so I could get over there and find out. I grabbed my sandals and buckled them up and told Momma where I was going. I crossed the street right in the middle since there's almost no traffic in Hobbs. I saw Brother Davis with a hammer in his hand. I'm not afraid to talk to him because he is nice and kind to kids. "Brother Davis, what is this tent going to be?" He said, "Vonnie, this is going to be a house of prayer. We are going to have a summer long revival with the folks in Hobbs getting saved and filled with the Holy Ghost. I'm calling it *God's House of Prayer Tent Revival*." He put his head back and closed his eyes and said, "Thank you, Jesus." I'm pretty sure he was thanking the Lord for his new Cadillac and his new tent.

I was trying to think, what would a tent revival be like? Is there a piano player? Do they have songbooks? And I hope I wouldn't have to listen to preaching! I got excited thinking about having a tent-church right across the street and something going on all summer long! I went straight home to tell my Momma and my Sissy *everything*.

I like going to church at Faith Pentecostal, but just for the music and the piano playing and not for the preaching. I always ask Momma if I can sit up close to the front so I can watch the most beautiful piano player in the world, Miss Janie Larue.

I plan to be just like Janie Larue because she plays at church and I think that makes God and Jesus like her special. Since I'm learning all about Hell, I am trying to be a really good Christian. I try to do what Brother Higgins says and what my Momma says. I am only 10, but I am already learning to play church songs and I hope I can stay on the *nice* side of God like janie Larue does. So along with our scales, chords and one new piece from John Thompson, our teacher, Mrs. Hays, assigns us a gospel song every week.

When we looked across the street next time, the tent was standing up nice and straight and I saw a Curtis Piano truck and two men rolling a brand-new piano inside the tent. I could hardly wait to get back over there to watch because any piano I ever see, I want to play it! I told Momma I just had to get back over there to try out that new piano, and she didn't stop me. After they got the piano rolled in, two more men were bringing in long benches for the crowd to sit on. This tent-church was going up fast!

Brother Davis was sweeping over by that new piano and I asked him, "Brother Davis, do you think I could try out your new piano?" I knew he would say yes, so I went over and touched the shiny, white keys. I ran my fingers up and down just feeling how smooth they were. I could smell the wood polished up so pretty. I sat down and I remembered to spread out my skirt around me, like Janie Larue does, and I played *Amazing Grace* just like in the songbook, using both my right and left hand. I didn't know it, but the workers had set their benches down and stopped to listen, and when I finished they clapped! I guess they didn't expect to hear such pretty playing from a kid!

I could have played all day, but Sissy stuck her head around the corner and yelled, "Vonnie, it's time to eat lunch!" When we were leaving, Brother Davis said, "Tell your Momma and Daddy to come on over to the Revival tonight. We have a fine preacher and his wife from out of town."

That afternoon every single thing got *better*! Sissy, Momma and me heard a loud racket and passing right in front of our house was Brother Davis, driving his new Cadillac real slow so everyone could hear what he was saying. He had what Momma calls a megaphone stuck out the window and he was driving all over town telling people about the Revival; "Revival meeting, tonight and every night, God's House of Prayer! Come and hear the Singing Smiths! Preaching and singing tonight!"

Then he would start all over again announcing the revival but his voice got softer and when he turned the corner, we could barely hear him. I was about to bust I was so excited! So that night, I begged my daddy to go and sure enough he went with me.

The tent was full of people all sitting down on the new benches. And there was a good piano player, a lady I didn't know. But the biggest and best surprise of all, a black and white accordion was sitting right there on the wood platform with its shiny white keys and little black buttons. I have seen them in the Sears catalog and they cost a lot of money, but I folded the page down because one day, I plan to buy one for myself.

When it was time for the special music, my favorite thing in the world, Sister Smith marched right across the wood platform in her fancy clothes, her high heels clacking when she walked. She bent down and picked up that big accordion without any trouble and put her arms through the straps and unfastened the buckles.

I never saw this before in my life, but people had drove their cars right up to the edge of the tent and parked. I guess they wanted to see what was going on but they didn't want to put on their nice clothes, or maybe like me they came for the special music. But with those loud-speakers going, people could hear the singing and preaching all over Hobbs!

Nobody was more excited than me! I wanted Sissy and everyone to see what came next. Brother Smith, Sister Smith's Preacher husband, came over to his wife and stopped to tune up his guitar, then he nodded to her and pretty soon she turned her hands sideways to play the little black and white keys, then she pulled the accordion back and forth pushing the black buttons with her other hand, and out came a beautiful sound! When she almost got the accordion closed up, why, then she remembered to keep pulling and pushing!

Then they leaned their heads close together and sang a song about Heaven, *Heaven, Happy Home Above*. He sang the melody and she sang the alto part. I could hardly sit still watching it! I listened to the words about heaven, but I couldn't take my eyes off Sister Smith. All that pulling and pushing and singing! She played on those little keys, pulling the other side back and forth, her fingers finding those buttons without ever looking, and all the time singing right along with her Preacher husband. When they finished, we stood up and clapped for them, and the people out in their cars honked their horns, they liked it so much! I decided this had to be the best tent revival that ever came to Hobbs, New Mexico!

The tent revival went on for two more weeks every single night, even Saturday. And I made sure to get myself over there to watch Sister Smith, singing with her Preacher husband and playing her accordion. Daddy went the next few nights but then he got too tired, so I went by myself and sat right on the front seat leaning forward, swinging my feet and waiting for Sister Smith and her accordion playing. When cars pulled up slow outside the tent with their lights shining in, they hurried to turn them off so they could be nice and polite. Then they just sat there in their cars waiting for the special music, just like me.

I didn't want them to go, but then after two weeks Brother and Sister Smith took their guitar and accordion and their fancy clothes and went off to Lovington to do more singing and preaching.

But the tent was still lighted up at night and Brother Davis and a few people kept right on trying to have church. It wasn't the same without the special singing and Sister Smith's accordion, but Momma and Daddy let me go over to the tent whenever I wanted. There are lots of places I am not allowed to go like movies or ball games or to the skating rink, but they never worried about me going to the tent revival. I guess they figured it was just fine and a safe place to be.

But after the Singing Smiths left, we kept having the Revival, and it turned out that Brother Davis wasn't a very good singer and he tried leading the songs, but there was no one to play the piano. I sat on the front seat just like always, and in the middle of everything, I raised my hand and spoke up and said, "Brother Davis, if you need a piano player, I sure will be glad to help you out." He was a little bit surprised, but then he said, "Sure, Vonnie, come on up."

I was sitting down a little ways from a big tall man that I decided to call the "Hallelujah Man." When I said I would play the piano, he jumped straight up from his seat and yelled, "Hallelujah!"

I stepped up on the wood platform, real excited to play that new piano again. My feet wouldn't quite reach the pedals so I sat on the edge of the bench and stuck my foot out as far as I could.

I told Brother Davis which songs I could play, and they had to be in the Key of C. I told him I was sure I could play *When We All Get to Heaven*. So, he asked people to turn to page number 99, and when it was time I just took off playing and left it up to the singers to catch up with me. We sang all three verses, and when we finished, I heard the Hallelujah man yell, "Hallelujah!"

I felt mighty grown up and proud when I jumped down off the wood platform. I sneaked out the side of the tent before the preaching started, since that is my most unfavorite part of church. When I got home, I couldn't wait to tell Momma and Daddy, and when they heard that I played for church over at the Revival, my Daddy grinned from ear to ear. My Momma looked up from her paper and said, "Well, dear, now that was really good practice for you."

Later when Momma was tucking Sissy and me in bed, she asked me, "Vonnie, was the *Hallelujah Man* there tonight?" "Yes, Momma," I said, almost falling asleep, "and he really likes my piano playing."

Funerals with Daddy

After church, Daddy didn't even take off his white shirt or tie when he ate his Sunday dinner. He was going to Mr. Sanders' funeral and he said I could go, too. Sissy never wants to go, but my Daddy goes to lots of funerals and I like going along. I know lots of other kids in the fourth grade and they've never been to one funeral in their whole life!

Daddy told Momma before church that his favorite customer, Mr. Sanders, died all of a sudden with a heart attack. Daddy had tears in his eyes. "Such a fine, friendly guy, and the best customer I've ever had," he said, pulling out his hanky and wiping his eyes. Daddy has fixed Mr. Sanders' cars for a long time. He drove a big blue Oldsmobile, and it's still sitting in Daddy's shop waiting to be fixed.

When Daddy finished the last bite of Momma's chocolate pie, he said, "OK, Skeedle Dumpling, get your shoes on." I like Daddy's special name for me. I wiggled my feet into my black patent leather shoes without even having to buckle them. I love how shiny they are. When I was real little, Momma says I tried to suck the toe of my patent leather shoe! To me they still look like Devil's Food cookies, the dark, shiny ones. Today, I got to wear my pink Sunday dress with lace in the shape of a heart on front. "I'm coming, Daddy!"

I love riding in the front seat with Daddy. Me and Sissy always have to sit in the back, but for funerals, I get to sit in the front. When I can't see out, I pull my knees under me and sit sideways. Today we are going to the Bethel Baptist Church.

Daddy took my hand and we walked right up close to the front.

The first three rows are always saved so the family can sit there. First thing, I always check for the casket, and sure enough, there it was right in the front. The funeral home people always put it there and they leave it open, with a nice cloth hanging over it. Today it is a light pink.

The family is sitting together, some with their arms around each other, and the first song is *Farther Along.* I sing loud along with Daddy since I know every word.

> *Farther Along, we'll know all about it,*
> *Farther Along, we'll understand why*
> *Cheer up my brothers, Live in the sunshine, we'll*
> *understand it all bye and bye...*

I know the words because it seems like the families always want to sing that song at funerals. When we finished singing, the preacher stood up and talked about Mister Sanders, and said what a good and kind man he was. Some people wiped their eyes, but they didn't cry like the last funeral Daddy took me to.

I have been to a lot of funerals and seen a lot of dead bodies even though I am just 10. I am curious about dead people and I want to know how they look. Sometimes, not being very tall, I used to have to tiptoe to barely get a look when all the people walk by the casket to say their goodbyes. Some people won't turn their heads to look inside at all and even look the other way. But I look!

My Daddy knows a lot of people from fixing their cars, and he has a lot of friends in Hobbs. So even if he barely knows someone, he says he feels his "duty" to go to the funeral and pay his last respects. And now that I'm 10, I'm tall enough to see inside the casket. When I was really little, Daddy sometimes lifted me up to see, and I was glad he did.

This is a quiet funeral, and I have been to some noisy ones. The last funeral Daddy took me to, there was lots of crying. It didn't bother me because I am used to people breaking down and crying at church when they get saved. Momma says they cry for joy and happiness, but I'm not sure.

I remember when I was only six years old and my step-grandpa died. My Grandma and even his kids called him "Mister Tom." My Momma didn't talk to him or call him anything. He sat in his big, easy chair over in the corner, and my grandma had to do everything for him, even shave him. "It's pure-dee *laziness* on his part," Momma said. So, she stared at him with hate in her eyes.

Mister Tom had three kids and my Grandma had three kids from her first husband, and by the time it was over, Grandma had nine children to cook for and feed! She was scrawny and tired all the time. My Momma didn't like him for that, but even worse, Mister Tom liked to hug on his grownup son's wives and pat them on the be-hind! I don't know if he ever tried that with my Momma, but I think she might have slapped him hard if he did. When we go to visit, my Momma leaves there as mad as a wet hen. Daddy usually says to her, "Try not to get riled up, Hon." But I don't think my Daddy liked him either.

When he *finally* died, we got the car packed with our Sunday clothes, and drove a long way to Texarkana, so we would be all ready for the funeral. We got to my Grandma's house and there was lots of cars around, and a wreath with big, black ribbons hanging on the front door. We walked around the back way and there was my Daddy's brothers and sisters standing on the porch, some of them I didn't know. Daddy hugged all of them and talked a few minutes then we went on in the house.

I looked in the living room. It was real dark in there with the shades pulled and everybody was whispering. Right there in the middle was the casket taking up almost the whole room. The casket was opened up and my daddy's stepsister Clara stood there crying. She said over and over, "Papa, I love you. I love you." And she wiped her eyes and moved over for us to see. I reached up for my Daddy's hand. Daddy didn't say a word or cry one tear when he bent over to look at his stepdad. He stood a long time just looking. Then he lifted me up so I could see, because I was little and only six. Mister Tom's face wasn't red anymore, it was white and chalky. He had on a shirt and a red bowtie, and his tie was crooked. But I sure wasn't going to fix it for him. All of a sudden, I was ready for Daddy to put me down!

The grownups were drinking coffee and talking real soft in the kitchen like you're supposed to do when somebody dies, so I went to look for my Grandma. But I couldn't find her anywhere. My Momma said later to Daddy she hoped Grandma would finally be able to get some rest, "She hasn't rested for 40 years and she sure needs it."

My Daddy never cried one tear that day or at the funeral, because I was watching him. When I heard that Mister Tom was mean to my Daddy and his brother, I decided I was glad he died! And I think my Momma was, too!

Sitting with Daddy and Momma and Sissy at the funeral, I was glad my Momma got her wish that he died. She won't ever have to worry what she might do if Mister Tom would ever try to pat her on the butt.

I keep right on going to funerals with my Daddy, but I am pretty sure I know at least one person who went straight to Hell.

My Grandma Clark and Mister Tom

When Rosemary told her brother, Thomas, about my Grandma Clark, a widow with three small children, he danced a little jig. He told his sister he sure did need a wife, and he said he was extra glad to know that my Grandma is a fine, Christian woman and would Rosemary please write this nice lady back!

Growing up, I didn't know about any of this. But my Daddy started telling us what happened to his Momma, and this is what he said. His real Papa, Grandpa Clark, took sick with the Flu, and "… in just a few days, my Papa was plumb gone", he said. I could see that after all this time, my Daddy was still sad about it. Daddy was only five years old.

That left his poor Momma with three little boys to feed and raise by herself. They lived in Arkansas, and my Grandma Clark thought she should stay put there because she had no place to go, and at least she could grow a garden for food. Her neighbors were kind, Daddy said, and in the winter, they brought over their home-canned food to share, and the men cut her some firewood. But Daddy said that wasn't enough food or help for my Grandma and her kids.

This is what happened next. My Grandma took in ironing for the town folk, but that still wasn't near enough money to feed and clothe her family. I guess Grandma Clark, my nicest Grandma, didn't know what to do next and she got more and more worried how she would feed her little boys.

So that's when she wrote to her friend, Rosemary in Kansas, and told her how bad things were with her husband dead and gone and three little children left to feed. Rosemary had lost track of my Grandma, and when she wrote her back, she told Grandma she was so sorry about her husband dying, that the same thing had happened to her brother, Thomas. His wife died and left him with three little kids. In her letter, Rosemary said her brother was a fine man, a preacher, part-time, called by God to carry the Gospel to the unsaved. Rosemary said maybe they would like to meet each other. When Thomas heard more about my Grandma Clark, he said yes! ... And that's when he danced his little jig, because he wanted to meet a nice woman to marry him and help him out with his kids.

Daddy said not only was his Momma a good, Christian woman, she was a good singer, too. After Grandma read Rosemary's letter, she thought it was really nice that somebody like this "Thomas" man cared, and she wondered if she might be able to help this poor preacher, a widower, both with his children and with his church work. Daddy said things were getting worse and Grandma was plumb wore out from trying to make ends meet. He said in those days, people usually farmed to make their living, but Grandma didn't own any land, and couldn't do work like that, anyway. Daddy said since things were getting worse and worse for Grandma, she thought maybe marrying this man was just the right thing to do.

So, Grandma sent a letter back to Rosemary saying that if her poor, sad brother was still interested, she would come to meet him. One of the neighbor ladies came over to help my Grandma pack up hers and the children's clothes; a few of her favorite things from her Momma, and a treasured picture of her dear, dead husband, William J. Clark. Her friend, Rosemary, sent her some money to buy the train tickets for her little family to ride all the way to Pin Oak, Kansas, to meet her brother. My Daddy, William J. Clark Jr., was the oldest and by then he was six, Mack was four, and the little one, Howie, was two. My Grandma Clark had never laid eyes on Rosemary's brother, but she knew he was supposed to be a good Christian man and even a preacher. She hoped she was doing the right thing.

Daddy said the next day her neighbor brought over her old horse and wagon and they heaved the big trunk onto the wagon, then my Grandma and the little boys climbed in. When they got to the train station, right there was a man taking pictures of people getting ready to board the train, and he snapped a picture of Grandma dressed in a hat and a long dress like they used to wear back then. In the picture, my Grandma was holding her little baby and beside Grandma was the trunk with all her worldly goods inside; and hanging on to her skirt was my Daddy and his brother, Mack.

Daddy said Grandma Clark's neighbor packed food for them to eat and he remembered taking naps on the seat of the train. When they finally arrived at Pin Oak, Kansas, my Grandma was in for a big surprise. There stood her new husband. He had a dirty old hat on, and three dirty, little kids stood beside him! He was twice as tall and twice as wide as my Grandma. He grinned big, and he reached down and picked up my Grandma like she was a kid, squeezed her hard and finally he set her back down on the ground.

I don't know what my Grandma Clark thought, but if that was me, I think I would grab my little boys and run back to that train. But she didn't and the next week they got married. Thomas told my Grandma, "Now that we are married, I expect you and your children to call me Mister Tom."

In just a few hours, my Grandma Clark had eight people to

cook and take care of. Mister Tom and his dirty little kids, and herself, and her own kids. Before it was over, my Grandma had seven more babies, but some of her babies died.

Later my Momma learned a lot more about my poor Grandma and how mean Mister Tom was to her. He believed he was God's messenger and supposably that meant he deserved special treatment. Everyone, even my Grandma had to do exactly like he told them, or they would be punished. When my Momma heard this, it made her so mad! My Grandma cooked and waited on him and everybody else, and she said, "Yes, Mister Tom, no, Mister Tom."

My Daddy said he wasn't allowed to go to school after he was 10, and Grandma's new husband made my Daddy and his brothers stay home from school to work on the farm. Mister Tom didn't think kids needed to go to school. And since he thought he was like God, he could teach them anything they needed to know. That made my Momma extra mad!

At Christmas and Easter, when we went to see them, Grandma ate her food standing up. All the other grownups sat around the table, but since Grandma was busy getting drinks and extra helpings for Mister Tom, she ate whenever she could. Once I told Momma I didn't have a place to sit at the table, so Mister Tom grinned and said to my Momma, "Just tell her to sit on her fist and lean back on her thumb." I didn't like him saying that because it doesn't make one bit of sense.

My Momma wasn't the only one who thought the way he treated people was wrong. That's why when he died and they had his funeral, I sat between my Momma and Daddy swinging my feet with my arms crossed and I wasn't one bit sad.

After Mister Tom died, Grandma moved to a pretty little house by herself right next door to her kids. Finally, she didn't have anybody she had to wait on and shave for every morning and there was nobody to boss her around and tell her what she could or couldn't do.

After Mister Tom died, my Grandma sang all the time. Once in a while she would throw up her hands and say, "Praise the Lord!" I know why my Grandma was happy and praising the Lord. It's because "somebody" was dead. And I didn't ask Momma, but I'm pretty sure she agrees.

Don't Be Kissing Boys in Cars

My friend, Kay Lynn's Daddy taught her how to drive, so she can take her Momma around to shop and pay the gas and electric bill. But some afternoons, they just get in the car and drive over to the Dairy Queen to have ice cream! Kay Lynn is already 15. Sometimes, I just know I'll never be older than 10!

Once you are a teenager at Faith Pentecostal Church you get to do all kinds of things. The boys and girls get to sit together at church, and if no one can see them, they hold hands or the boys put their arm around their girlfriend. The girls whisper and giggle and sometimes they pass notes, or they file each other's fingernails. Every Thursday night the youth group has *Teens Night Out*, and no one my age is ever allowed!

If I could change one thing, I would be a teenager overnight and I wouldn't have to get left out of everything. In the winter I could go along for their wiener roast at the Phillips Petroleum Park where there is a blazing hot flare burning all the time! It is so *hot* and so *bright*, my Daddy says it's at least 75 feet tall, up there burning the gas off, trying to cover up the nasty smell from all the oil wells. But it still stinks! A lot of people say Hobbs is the stinkiest town they've ever been to!

So, the Phillips people keep that screaming, hot fire going day and night to cover up the awful smell. That flame is bigger than a pickup truck! When I saw it, it looked like it was bright daytime, but it was really night! It can keep you warm and you won't even need your coat, but if you get too close, it will nearly bake your skin. The teenagers don't mind, and I wouldn't mind either, if only I could get invited to go!

Our youth group at church named themselves "Hobbs Youth for Jesus." They even made up their own song. The words are, *Every day is new, all our skies are blue, walking on the King's Highway.* I know *all* the words.

I just hate being 10 years old. Another reason is because teenagers in Hobbs get a student driver's license when they are only 15! Kay Lynn is five years older than me, but she drives herself and her Momma to church and everywhere. But then, one night Kay Lynn showed up at church with her new boyfriend, Sammy Jr. They sat as far back as they could and Sammy Jr. put his arm around Kay Lynn's seat, and I already know Preacher Higgins does *not* like that! I was watching them from the front, because I knew our preacher would say something about it, and sure enough he did!

So when Brother Higgins noticed Sammy Jr.'s arm, we sang another song, and then he went over to the microphone and asked everybody to bow their heads and close their eyes and I didn't bow my head and I didn't close my eyes because I wanted to see just what would happen; and then he moved over and spoke real serious and polite into the microphone and said, "Will the young man please remove his arm from around the young lady?" And then he just waited. I was watching close and I think Kay Lynn and Sammy Jr. couldn't believe Brother Higgins would even care about his arm around the back of the seat. So, we waited and waited, and I didn't know what would happen. I was getting so nervous just watching. Finally, Sammy Jr. caught on and he moved his arm! I could hardly catch my breath I was so embarrassed for them, especially Sammy Jr. who has never even been to our church before! I would *hate* to be them and my face would be so red and I would never, ever come back to Faith Pentecostal!

So, Preacher Higgins, he said some little prayer and then we went on with church like nothing awful had just happened. That was the same night Brother Higgins decided to preach to the young people. He said, "Well, the Lord is leading me to switch gears and preach to the youth." I wanted to be sure and listen since it will be good for me to know what to do my own self when I'm older.

Brother Higgins said to open our Bibles to 2nd Corinthians, which I did. He read from the Bible and said how bad and how serious it would be for a good, clean Christian girl or boy to go off and marry somebody who is a sinner. He said the apostle Paul tells us not to be "unequally yoked together with an unbeliever." He said, "A wife or husband who isn't saved will drag you and your children down to Hell right along with them!" Listening to him, I knew I would be awful scared myself to fall in love with a sinner.

Then Brother Higgins looked even more serious and his voice changed, and he looked like maybe he was about to preach at a funeral. He read some more scriptures and said, "The Apostle Paul made it clear about the Sins of the flesh." He said young people are especially tempted, wanting to sin and give over to their "carnal and sinful desires." Brother Higgins' face was red, and he coughed a little bit talking about their fleshly desires. He wasn't yelling like he does sometimes. I think he was worried especially about the "young ladies." That's what he called them. He said the devil would be putting them to the test on whether they would give in to temptation and be kissing and necking in cars. And it would be "up to the young ladies to decide to stay true, and keep their bodies clean and pure for their husbands," he said.

He asked Janie Larue, sitting at the piano to play the song *Keep Me True, Lord Jesus*. Then he read the words to the song.

> *"There's a race that I must run.*
> *There are victories to be won.*
> *Give me power, every hour, to be true."*

So, Janie played *Keep Me True, Lord Jesus*, and Brother Higgins still talking in his funeral voice asked the young people, mostly the young ladies, I think, to be making a decision whether or not they are willing to put God first to stay pure and holy.

Right then, I decided being only 10 years old was just fine, since I don't know if I could make a promise to Brother Higgins that I won't ever kiss a boy in a car. That Janie Larue is so lucky and probably real glad she could go play the piano and nobody would know if she made a promise about kissing boys or not. She was busy playing the piano and that was what she got to think about instead. One day, I hope I will be busy playing and not have to think about sin or being in Hell forever! People will think I'm an *extra* good Christian because I play the piano at Faith Pentecostal.

Next, Brother Higgins asked us to stand up. "Now, it's time for the young people to come forward and decide whether or not they will promise to be true to Jesus!" I thought about Kay Lynn with her boyfriend sitting way in the back. She was probably trying to decide whether she would kiss her new boyfriend in the car or not. What Brother Higgins was saying is if she did go ahead and kiss him, she would be giving in to the devil. But Kay Lynn didn't go forward and promise Brother Higgins anything! She just stayed back there with her boyfriend, Sammy Jr. I was happy for her and scared for her all at the same time!

There are at least two big reasons I am practicing the piano so hard: Number one, because I am such a good piano player, and number two, if I am busy playing at church, just like Janie Larue, I'll be excused from making promises I can't keep about kissing boys in cars.

Miss Bello and the Mother's Day Belts

I didn't know how an old toothbrush could help us make a belt, but Miss Bello my fourth-grade teacher, said we were doing a special art project for Mother's Day and to bring an old toothbrush from home. She said we were going to do some belt making, using a toothbrush for a giant needle. Miss Bello reached in her desk drawer and pulled out a belt made with yellow cord and tied in different places with a buckle at the end. She said once we were done, we could give it to our mom or our grandma or wear it to hold our jeans up, or put it in the trash. Some of the boys snickered and laughed, thinking about wearing a yellow belt to hold up their Wrangler jeans.

The next morning, I remembered to get the worn-out toothbrush from under the sink that me and Sissy use to clean off our shoes and I stuck it in my satchel. After lunch Miss Bello held up a cut off toothbrush with some cord threaded through the hole in the bottom. She had cut the brush end off and looped the yellow cord in the hole at the other end. She showed us how we could use it to draw the cord in and out like a big sewing needle making loops and knots.

Miss Bello is tall and skinny and dark-skinned. Daddy says she is Indian, and I sure don't know but Miss Bello is nice to all the kids and we are extra lucky she makes art with us. She told us to gather around the worktable while she handed out the yellow cord. She picked up the big green paper cutter with the heavy metal blade and set it down in front of her. She looked around and told us to stand back. Then she put Jimmy Don's old toothbrush right under the metal handle. Miss Bello gritted her teeth, making a face and pushed down as hard as she could on the handle. Finally, the metal arm went down with a loud whack and the two ends of the toothbrush broke right in half. She cut several more toothbrushes for the first group. Then she took those kids over to the corner to help them thread the cord so they could start making their belts.

Several of us kids didn't have our toothbrushes cut and we got tired of just standing around. It didn't seem to me like cutting them in half would be hard to do, so I said I thought we should put our toothbrushes on the paper cutter and do the job ourselves. I laid my toothbrush under the blade and was ready to bring the handle down and just then Dee Dee stopped me, "Wait, Vonnie, you don't have it set right!" So, I moved over and she put the middle of the toothbrush right under the steel blade. I moved back to the paper cutter and reached up pulling the handle down as hard as I could, but nothing happened. The big blade just sat on the toothbrush. Then I decided to try again and this time I put both of my hands on the metal handle and pushed as hard as I could so that my feet lifted up off the floor! It took a second before the metal blade cut the toothbrush in half, and then there was a loud wack! I didn't know it, but my middle finger was too close to the blade. I looked down and saw blood spurting all over the paper cutter and dripping onto the floor.

Dee Dee screamed, "Miss Bello, Miss Bello!" "Come quick, Vonnie is hurt!" Miss Bello jumped up and came flying over. When she saw the blood, she said, "Oh my God, Vonnie, what have you done!" My finger hurt so bad, and I saw all the blood but all I could do was stand and stare at it.

But then Miss Bello dropped the toothbrush in her hand and pulled me by my other hand down the hall with blood dripping on the green tile floor and on my plaid skirt. "Hurry up, Vonnie, walk *faster*, we've got to get you to the hospital!" I followed her past the office and when Mr. Drew saw my finger he stopped in his tracks, then he ran over to get some paper towels stacked on the nurse's table. He met Miss Bello at the door and handed her the paper towels. "I'll call you from the hospital," she said. She pulled me out the front door toward her car. Mr. Drew ran after us, calling, 'Be careful, Miss Bello! I'll call Vonnie's Mom!'

Miss Bello dragged me to her little red coupe, put me in the front seat and shut the door for me. She started the car and jerked it into gear. I looked down to see the red pool of blood under my finger on the paper towel spreading to the edges. Looking at the end of my finger, dangling and bleeding I felt dizzy. "Oh my God, Vonnie," Miss Bello said when she looked over. I held still because I was feeling a little sick.

At the hospital, Miss Bello pulled right in the emergency drive where the ambulances were. She left her door wide open and ran to help me out. I stumbled along after her. We passed by the office and when the nurse saw my finger, she stood up and came around to put me on a bed. I climbed on, shoes and all. The doctor came in so I held out my hand so he could see. The end of my finger dangled off the top. I couldn't think of anything to say so I just laid there. I saw the Doctor's needle slide into my finger, so I turned my head to the wall. I felt him pulling my finger this way and that way, sewing me up. I didn't want to look so I closed my eyes.

When I woke up and opened my eyes, I had a big white bandage taped all the way from my finger up around my wrist and standing in front of me was my Momma.

"Well, Vonnie," Momma said, "you worked your finger over really good. They had to take 12 stitches to get it fixed."
"But you are going to be all right," she said, nodding her head.

"Can I still play the piano, Momma?"
"Yes, you can."

"And Momma, will I be able to type when I'm all grown up,"
I asked.

"Yes, you can type," she said, "you sure can."

That night, waiting for my Daddy to come home, I couldn't
wait to tell him every single thing that happened. Momma told
me to go lay down on the couch and rest, and I tried but I kept
remembering more things to tell Momma, and one was that
Miss Bello took the Lord's name in vain at least three times,
before we got to the hospital. Finally, Momma said, "Well,
Vonnie, I guess you're just too worked up to be laying down."
So, I got up and sat at the table waiting for Daddy, my poor,
bandaged hand propped on the table.

When I went back to school the next day, everyone wanted to
know if they amputated my finger since there was so much
blood dripping down the hall. After it happened, Sissy saw the
blood and heard the stories from my friends. She was pretty
scared I had died.

That next morning, I brought a note back to school that I had
wrote to Miss Bello the night before with my good hand. I told
her I was sorry for all the trouble, and I would help her clean
her car up from the blood if she wanted. She thought for a
minute, then she said, "Thanks, Vonnie, but you have done
enough. You have done quite enough."

KNEW Radio Station and Me!

Janie Larue got sick last year with rheumatic fever and when she finally got well and came back to church, everybody said her piano playing was the best in all of Lea County. But I say she's the best in the whole world!

Momma lets me sit up front so I can watch Janie play, but if I don't behave, she sends Sissy up to get me and I have to go back and sit right next to her. I don't like for her to do that because then everybody at church knows I was misbehaving.

I am 10, almost 11, and I play my piano pieces for anybody I can. I am learning songs from the *Favorites* gospel songbook we keep in our piano stool, mostly in the Key of C or F or G since they are easy. Brother Davis is the preacher who got rich enough to buy a big tent, and he keeps his revival going every night across the street from us. If no one else shows up to play, he is glad I can help him out. Daddy and Momma let me go. And it's a good thing I am practicing as much as I am!

Our piano teacher, Mrs. Hays, is teaching me and Sissy how to make chords in the major keys. I am learning about octaves, scales and chord inversions. It makes it easier to see what Janie Larue is playing in her left hand. She reaches down in the bass and if we are singing in the key of F, she plays an F with her pinkie, then she comes back up to the middle and matches it up with an F chord. It is a little like oom-pa-pa and all the time she keeps the melody going with her right hand, making chords there, too. She is the best in the whole world!

Watching her I get so excited! It doesn't look that hard. I crane my neck to watch her, and one day after church I asked Janie to show me more chords. She motioned for me to sit beside her on the piano bench. Janie Larue is my night and day idol, so I scooted over next to her and took a deep, sweet breath of her perfume. She smelled just like my Momma's hand lotion.

Janie took my left hand and put my pinkie on the low F, then after I played that she moved my hand up toward the middle of the keyboard to make the F chord. We tried putting the right-hand melody with the chords and I got more and more excited! When we finished, Janie gave me a squeeze and said, "You keep practicing, Vonnie!" After church, I went straight to the piano without even taking my coat off, and practiced over and over putting chords to songs in the key of C and then F. Then later I tried playing chords with songs out of the *Favorites* songbook.

I worked until Momma made me stop and eat Sunday dinner, but then I practiced some more. Finally, I could keep the melody going all the time making my chords in the left hand, and it sounded bea-u-tiful! My Daddy, he looked up from his Sunday paper and said, "That sounds real good, Skeedle Dumpling."

The very next afternoon, our brand-new telephone rang. It was only the second time it rang since we just got the phone that morning. A telephone man driving a pickup truck with Southwestern Telephone Company printed on his shirt came to install it. He had on a leather belt crammed with tools and on the other side of his blue shirt right above his pocket it said in cursive, "Donny." Me and Sissy, we were so excited! We never thought our Momma would get us a phone, but she did!

Mr. Donny worked outside our front window, with Sissy and me watching everything, and then he drilled a hole for the cord to come in through the wall. I could hardly stand it waiting for him to finish because I had a lot of people to call! Then he came inside the house and took a brand-new telephone from a cardboard box. He set it on the end table, then he knelt down by the baseboard and pulled the cord through from outside and connected it to our new phone with me and Sissy standing right beside him. Sissy said she wanted to be the first one to make a call and I said, no, I want to be the first one! Finally, Momma said, "Girls, move away and let Donny work!" When he was finished, Mr. Donny stood up and put the tools back in his leather belt. He said, "All right, Mrs. Clark, you now have your own telephone and you can call anyone in the United States of America. Also, you can call anyone here in Hobbs for free and talk as long as you want, you just dial the number." He put a little Directory beside the new phone, and on the front, it said, "Hobbs, New Mexico, 1955."

So, you can see how excited we were to get a real phone call in the afternoon. It was our preacher, Brother Higgins, calling. Momma told him, "Well, yes, we were all feeling fine," then after listening for a while she said, "Well I don't know why she couldn't help you out," and she kept looking over at me. "All right, we'll see what we can do, ...yes, I'll tell her. Bye."

When she hung up, Momma said, "Well, Vonnie it looks like you're going to get a chance to play for the Lord on the radio! Brother and Sister Higgins are going to have a radio program starting next Saturday. Janie Larue can't get a ride to town every Saturday, so they want you to play the piano for them to sing their duets."

"Me? Momma?" I said, trying to catch my breath. I know my eyes were bugging out, I was so surprised. And excited!

"Yes, Vonnie, now you can do something real nice for the Lord."

"Well, I hope I get real famous, Momma," I said. I couldn't hardly believe I was going to be on the radio playing for the Lord. Maybe I really can be excused from Hell!

So, Monday afternoon after school, Momma took me over to the parsonage to practice. Beside the front door was a little sign that said, "The Gospel of Jesus Christ Spoken Here." I like Sister Higgins a lot better than Brother Higgins. Sometimes I sit beside her at church because she sits up front, too, but not because she wants to have a look at Sister Annie's goiter.

Momma left me there with Sister Higgins and I went over to her beautiful piano. She put a piece of sheet music on the piano, a song I'd never seen. It was called *No One Ever Cared for Me like Jesus*. She played the melody for me and hummed a little, then I did the same. I practiced a little bit, and I asked her if I could take the music home with me. I promised I would have it learned by Saturday afternoon in time for the radio program. I practiced way past my bedtime, and Momma and Daddy never said a word. Now, I'm pretty sure since I'll be playing the piano on the radio, I'll make it to Heaven!

On Saturday, playing on the radio was all I could think about! I put on my best church clothes. Momma said it wasn't necessary, after all it was just the radio, and no one could see me. I was waiting around, dancing a jig, I was in such a hurry to play *on the air*. Finally, it was time to go, so Momma drove me to the radio station. On the building are the letters KNEW on the front. I had never been inside. When I was a little, I thought there were tiny people living and talking to each other inside our radio. I wondered how they got their food or used the bathroom since they never came out. I don't believe that anymore, but I do plan to find out how the radio really works.

Momma dropped me off early to practice the duet before the radio program. I walked through a hall and looked inside a room with a big window. The room was mostly empty but then I saw a piano and bench, a couple of folding chairs and a big clock on the wall. Brother Higgins smiled and waved. He stood in front of a microphone and Sister Higgins sat in a chair. I had learned that song just fine without a bit of trouble! In fact, I almost had it memorized. They got around the piano and I played the first few measures, then they began to practice the song. Brother Higgins stopped and coughed a lot. His throat was sore from preaching so loud I'm pretty sure, but once they got started, they sure sounded pretty together, her soft alto voice, and him singing the melody.

Right across the hall from our big window a man was sitting at a desk wearing earphones. Above the door inside our room was a little glass box with the words, "ON AIR." I found out they were going to light that thing up the second it was time to start. Thinking about it, I got scared. Now I *had* to do this whether I wanted to or not! It was too late to back out!

Brother Higgins told me what would happen. I would start the radio program by playing, *It is No Secret What God Can Do.* He will give me a signal when it's time, he said. Then, after that, he would start talking to introduce himself and go on from there. At the end of the program, I was supposed to play the same song again until he gave me the signal that we were all finished. It is such an easy song that I can play it by memory. That was supposed to be the first thing to happen once the ON AIR sign lighted up. Little ol' me, *Vonnie Clark*, will start off the KNEW radio program!

When the minute hand was about to reach 4 o'clock, we got in our places waiting without making a single sound, except that my heart was pounding! No coughing or sneezing, and I got ready and put my fingers on the very first notes of the song. Brother Higgins had his eyes glued to the man across the hall with the earphones ... 10 seconds, then ... five seconds then the ON AIR sign lighted up, and there I was, everybody waiting on me to start, and Brother Higgins pointing straight at me. So, I started playing my very first notes in public, and people all over Hobbs and Lea County and maybe people all over the world were listening!

Then I quieted down my playing while Brother Higgins introduced us, and "Miss Vonnie Clark is at the piano" he said. He talked about where our church was located at 816 East Pine, and he mentioned the address several times, so nobody would forget where to go. He said, "You will receive a great blessing if you come and visit Faith Pentecostal Church", but he wasn't hollering like usual since that would sound bad on the radio. Then he announced their duet, and I played the introduction and they started singing *No One Ever Cared for Me Like Jesus*. By then, I was just a little bit nervous, but I remembered not to cough or make a sound until we were finished.

Brother Higgins gave a real short sermon, since that's all the time he had. He talked to the "people out in radio-land" like they were his good friends. He said that if folks were listening who didn't go to church, he believed that worshipping God with the good church folks at Faith Pentecostal could change their lives. He finished up, and gave me the signal to play, so I ended up our radio program by playing *It Is No Secret*. The ON AIR sign went dark and we were done. And then, I just *had* to cough!

They drove me back home and both of them told me I did a real fine job, and they plan to keep having these radio programs every Saturday afternoon, and they sure hope I can help them out.

"Momma! I did it! I played on the radio!" I hollered, running in the house slamming the screen door after me. "Could you hear me? Did you and Daddy listen?" "Yes," she said, "when Sissy ran to get Daddy, he stopped what he was doing at the shop and we all listened right here by the radio." "It was real nice," she said, nodding her head, and that was a big compliment because Momma doesn't brag. Then Daddy peeked in the room and gave me a beaming smile.

"Momma, will I be famous now?" I asked.
"Nah, Vonnie. This is a small town, and nobody famous ever came out of Hobbs. But you did fine, and you helped out when you were needed."

"Don't you worry, Skeedle Dumpling, it was bea-u-tiful. You played like an Angel," Daddy said with a big smile. When I climbed into bed that night, I was pretty sure that I will be famous. And playing on the radio, is a real good start.

Granny Jenkins and the Shop Fire

It was almost Christmas, so Sister Higgins asked my Momma to be in the Christmas play at Faith Pentecostal. Momma doesn't pretend or play games with Sissy and me, so I wasn't sure she could do it. Momma's part was to pretend to be "Granny Jenkins", an old lady waiting at a train station to go visit her sister for Christmas. Momma let Sissy and me come along and watch the practices, "as long as you behave", she said. Daddy stayed working at his auto shop.

For her costume Momma put on an old shawl and borrowed some wire glasses, then she pulled her hair back in a little bun. And she had brought a suitcase from home. So, they had Momma sit down on a bench under a cardboard sign that said, "Train Station." Since Momma couldn't knit, she rolled up some yarn into a ball while she said her lines. When her turn came her voice was nice and loud so everyone could hear. Sitting humped over in her shawl wearing her glasses, I almost believed it was Granny Jenkins myself! She talked about how late the train was and already it was close to midnight. Then she pulled some more yarn up and kept rolling it.

We heard some noise, and someone clanged a bell behind the curtains when the pretend train finally came. Getting off the train dressed in old-fashioned clothes was a man and a woman. He carried a suitcase and she walked slow, her belly big and round. When I saw them better, it was just Darlene and Chester Hill, pretending to be tired and wore out from all their traveling. In the story, it was almost time for her to have her baby and since it was so late, Granny Jenkins, my Momma, said maybe she should cancel her trip and give them a place to stay for the night. That reminded me of Mary and Joseph when there was no room at the inn. They smiled and thanked Granny Jenkins. There they all were, in the pretend train station with my Momma looking like a nice Granny. I was just loving this play, and it seemed so real but it was really just a practice.

Right then, I looked around and my Uncle Howie came yelling and running from the back of the church, calling out Momma's name to tell her that Daddy's garage was on fire! In fact, we had to come quick! It was "going up in flames right now!"

Momma wasn't scared because she had trouble believing a word of it, so me and Sissy didn't know if it was even true. But before we got close, almost two blocks away, we could see the fire! Daddy's whole garage was blazing, and flames were shooting all the way up the sides! I didn't know if Momma was believing it was real or not, but I sure was! The firemen were working hard with their hoses blasting water back and forth into the fire. People stopped their cars in the middle of the street and got out just to look.

Sometimes, I don't know why, but when Momma is scared, she laughs. She giggled and said, "I just can't believe this!" But then I noticed that we hadn't seen my Daddy anywhere, and he might be inside the garage! I screamed, "Where is Daddy, Momma?!" I could hardly catch my breath, I was so scared. Then I pulled away to go looking for him, but Momma held onto my arm and wouldn't let go. "Momma," I screamed, "let me go!!"

Just then Daddy came from behind a truck and ran over when he saw Momma and Sissy and me standing out in the street. He was scared, too, I could tell. But I was so glad that he was safe I ran over and threw my arms around him, and so did Sissy. He looked at Momma and said, "It's all gone! Everything is gone," he said with tears in his eyes. Momma put her arms around Daddy and they just stood there watching. There was nothing else they could do.

That night when the firemen left and we finally came inside the house, I looked out my window across to where Daddy's shop had been. There was nothing there and I could see all the way to the streetlight. I could still smell smoke and burning tires. Usually when I looked out at night, I could see Daddy's garage standing nice and tall, the shop my Daddy built so he could support our family. But now, the ground is flat except for a pile of Daddy's melted tools. I didn't know where we would get enough money now for our food and clothes. I felt tears running down my cheeks.

Sissy and me laid in bed listening to Momma and Daddy and Uncle Howie talking in the kitchen. I felt so sorry that my Daddy lost his shop. I know I will miss peeking in anytime I want to see what Daddy is working on. He always stops what he is doing and he looks up and gives me a big smile. I know what he would say. He would say, "Skeedle Dumpling! What have you been up to?"

I think my very best gift this Christmas will be having my Daddy safe and sound sitting around the Christmas tree with Momma, Sissy and me just like always. I can't think of a bigger or better present in the whole world *even* if we don't get any other presents!

The next day, right there on the front page of the Hobbs Daily News-Sun was a picture of my Daddy's shop with flames shooting high in the sky and the firemen standing there with their hoses trying hard to save my Daddy's shop, but they just couldn't do it. The shop is gone now, but having my Daddy safe is the best thing in the world.

Lipstick and Miss Paula

One Sunday, Paula Winters decided to come to Faith Pentecostal Church with her husband, Floyd. I never saw anybody like Paula Winters at our church. I thought she came right straight from Hollywood! I couldn't stop staring at her. Miss Paula has blond hair cut real short and pretty, and she has long, black eyelashes and bright red lipstick, and her lipstick is the best part!

Preacher Higgins says lipstick is a really bad sin. But me? I want to wear lipstick more than anything in the whole world. I need to know if it would make me pretty. It looks soft and creamy and I'm nearly sure it tastes good. My fourth-grade teacher, Miss Bello, wears lipstick every day and she never forgets, because in the morning as soon as I take my coat off and hang it up, I always check to see. My Aunt Beth in Texas wears lipstick, too. But the church ladies at Faith Pentecostal are not allowed to wear lipstick or earrings because they might go right to Hell if they do.

On Saturdays, when we get our chores done, Momma gives Sissy and me money to spend in town. We can go all by ourselves, so we walk to Woolworth's where my friend Annie works on Saturdays, and she is just 15 years old! For fifty cents you can buy a diamond ring, ribbons for your hair, candy or lipstick. I always go to the lipstick counter first just to look, even though I can't buy it. The tubes are little, almost like toy lipstick. They have Pure Pink, Delicate Orange, and Racy Red. But I'm not allowed to buy it even for playing and pretending. "No reason to tempt yourself, Vonnie," Momma says. But if I could, I would always buy Racy Red.

Sometimes Momma and my Aunt Mindy talk about how they wish they could wear lipstick again like they did before they got saved. So, I asked her, "Why can't church ladies wear earrings and lipstick?" Momma thought a minute and said, "Well, Vonnie, in the New Testament, St. Paul says women are not supposed to adorn themselves." She didn't say why not. But no matter how I try, I can't stop loving lipstick and I wish Momma would just decide it's a silly rule.

The next time we went to Lubbock, I watched my Aunt Beth put her lipstick on. She took out her gold tube of lipstick and her tiny, little mirror. She held her mirror in one hand and rolled up the lipstick with the other. It was as red as the roses in Grandma P.'s front yard. My Aunt Beth looked in her mirror and stretched out her lower lip and smeared lipstick from side to side. Then slow and careful, she put the lipstick in the middle of her top lip smearing one side then the other. She mashed her lips together and made a little smacking sound when she finished. With her brown eyes and black hair and her lips nice and red, she looked just like a movie star! And it's hard to believe that she is a sinner, she is so sweet and nice.

But that Sunday, when Miss Paula and her husband Floyd, came to church, Brother Higgins, after he finished preaching, he asked Janie Larue to go to the piano and play softly, *Are You Washed in the Blood*. He was putting his coat on and clearing his throat. He sounded a little bit hoarse after preaching and hollering. Brother Higgins got his coat on and went back over to the microphone, "And now, folks, once again we come to the most important part of the church service when sinners have a chance to come to God." He said he was hoping anyone who was still living in sin would come forward, ask forgiveness and, "turn your whole life around to serve the Lord." He waited a little bit then he got real serious, frowning, and he said in his funeral voice, "Folks, you *need* to make this important decision today, since tomorrow might be too late!"

I was hoping whoever it was still living in sin, would just go ahead and come forward and get saved, so we could go home. But then, maybe Brother Higgins was talking to *me*! Maybe it's a sin to even *want* to wear lipstick. He was looking right at me when he said, "Every sinner needs to come to God, and tomorrow may be too late. Don't think you can get to Heaven riding on your Momma's shirt tail!"

I never even thought of such a thing, and anyway, how could you *hold on*, all the way up to Heaven? Thinking about going to Hell and those flames that won't ever go out, I felt so scared, but I didn't want to cry because then people would think I'm a sinner for sure. But what if I'm not really saved?

I just hate this part of church when we're all standing and waiting, and everybody is feeling bad and probably scared just like me. I looked around to see if there were lots of strangers and sinners Brother Higgins was talking to about getting saved, but only Miss Paula and Floyd were new.

Brother Higgins put his head down and closed his eyes, then he just stepped back, holding his Bible with his eyes closed. I looked over and Paula Winters was wiping her eyes heading down to the front, and when she got there, she knelt down at the altar trying to get saved before it was too late. Brother Higgins asked the ladies to come down and pray with her. Then all the grownups went to the altar. Me and Sissy, we didn't go. We probably should have. Sometimes, Momma tells us we have to go down to the altar to pray, so I go but I don't know what to tell the Lord. But Miss Paula's husband, Floyd, he didn't go either. He waited back at his seat. Later, he told our Preacher that he didn't think he needed to get saved.

Momma said Mr. and Mrs. Winters moved to Hobbs from Dallas where Miss Paula owned a beauty shop. She is tall and skinny, just like my Momma wants to be. Miss Paula looks different than any woman I've ever seen, and someone told Momma that she used to be a model in a magazine.

People wondered if Miss Paula would start letting her hair grow long like all the church ladies do. None of the ladies at Faith Pentecostal will cut their hair because of what St. Paul said, except for my Momma, Millie Faye. I think the other ladies are scared they will be sinning, so they keep their hair long. Most all the church ladies pull their hair tight and roll it up in a knot. But my Momma says she doesn't think God wants young, pretty women to go around looking awful, so she decided to do what she wants to about her hair.

Miss Paula keeps coming to church, but she still paints her lips bright red, and it is extra pretty! She told Momma, "Why, I don't think Jesus gives a hoot about lipstick or hair and I'm not fixing to change my appearance just because I got saved at Faith Pentecostal Church!" So, Miss Paula, she keeps cutting and bleaching her hair and people at Faith Pentecostal leave Miss Paula alone. I don't think I'll be brave enough to wear lipstick when I grow up. I'll be too scared. The only other lady at church who can break the rules is Sister Annie and she doesn't seem scared or worried about breaking rules.

I am proud Sister Annie is my special friend. Her goiter still looks like someone put an extra big wad of something on her neck. But it doesn't bother me, and I like looking. Sometimes I can't stop thinking about that goiter. I take my little cousin, Nannie, over to look at Sister Annie before church starts. Sister Annie is always nice to us and I like when she calls me "Darling." She wears her little gold earrings and lipstick even though it is a bad sin, but she doesn't worry like I do. I wish I could be more like Sister Annie and not worry about sinning and going to Hell.

I like writing about Sister Annie, and here is some more stuff about her. She is a white lady and pretty old. People at church don't know what to think about her "Negro" son. They talk about Sister Annie and her son. Some people say he's not really her son, but no one really knows. He brings her to church, walks her to her seat, but then he leaves and just waits in the car. He was the only Black person I *ever* saw come to church. But mostly, I don't care what Sister Annie does and I will keep writing about her because I think she's the best Christian of all. I like her because she keeps on wearing her lipstick and calling me "Darling."

Emanuel, Mr. B., and the Paddle

My best friend in the fourth grade is Carla Mendez. Sissy and me have blue eyes, and my Momma does, but Carla has big brown eyes and long eyelashes. My other best friend, Connie, has red hair and freckles, but Carla's skin is tan and smooth, like she has been swimming at the Hobbs City pool every day.

Just about everybody I know in Hobbs is white, except for the "Negroes" that live over on their side of town. There are two Mexican families living in our neighborhood. I think that makes some of the white people mad, and I keep hearing they want the Mexicans to go back to Mexico or maybe go on to the other side of town. But my Momma and Daddy don't mind and Momma says when she passes by Carla's house, "they have the nicest, neatest yard on the block, better than anybody's." My Daddy is too busy to make a nice yard.

I brought Carla to my house one day walking home from school. She came inside to meet my Momma and Daddy. Daddy shook her hand and said, "Mucho gusto, Carla. Cómo te va?" She smiled and said, "Mucho gusto. Estoy bien, Señor." Me and Sissy couldn't believe how Daddy spoke to Carla using words we had never heard! "Daddy, where did you learn those words?" I asked. "I lived in El Paso, Texas, when I was growing up right near the border. My very best friends were Mexican, and I still think about them to this day."

Momma lets me take the long way home so I can walk with Carla to her house. She lives with her two Aunties. Her Momma and Daddy still live in Mexico with her four brothers and sisters.

I love Carla's house! The rooms are a little bit dark except for candles burning. On the walls in the living room and dining room, there are little shelves with candles and statues. Carla said they are "nichos." The one I like best is Mary and the baby Jesus. I have never seen anything like this in somebody's house. It is so pretty!

I want to have nichos in our house with candles burning. Maybe Momma will get us some. When I told Momma about them, she said, "Carla's aunts must be Catholic, and Catholics have a lot of statues." That's a church I never heard of, but I decided right then that when I grow up and have my own house, I will have one of those nichos in every single room, even if I still go to Faith Pentecostal Church, and I probably will be so I can play the piano for Brother Higgins.

At our church we don't mention anything about Mary except at Christmas with the Baby Jesus, because at our church women don't matter as much as men. God and Jesus, the preachers and the deacons, they are important. And Brother Higgins says he and the deacons, they are the ones that keep the church going.

After Carla came to meet our family, Sissy told us about a "Mexican boy in class named Emanuel." His nickname is "Manuel." She said she felt sorry for him because she thinks Mr. B. hates him. Mr. B., Sissy's sixth grade teacher, has white hair and a red face and he is the biggest man at Hobbs Elementary.

I think Mr. B. wants the "Mexicans to go back to Mexico," or at least "go live on *their* side of town," Sissy said at breakfast. "One day," Sissy said, "Mr. B. got so mad at Manuel, he picked him up and flung him to the floor."

I could feel my cheeks getting hot, I felt so mad. I said, "If he did that to me, I would tell the police and they would put him in jail! I hope no one ever treats my friend Carla mean like that, just because of her dark skin."

I guess Mr. B. must have been especially mad that day, the way he screamed at Manuel. Sissy said he got his wooden paddle off the hook, and as loud as he could he yelled for Manuel to get ready because he was going to "Get It!" At our school, if a kid is going to get paddled, the teacher is supposed to call for a witness. Mr. B. shoved Manuel all the way to the front door yelling and called him a "stupid, little wetback." He looked back and told Ronnie Wayne to go next door and ask our teacher, Mr. Moore, to meet him outside.

Sissy said her class could see everything out the barracks windows. Mr. Moore came outside to watch and while he was waiting for Manuel to get his licks, he took a cigarette out of his pocket and lighted it up. Mr. B. got behind Manuel when he bent over, with his paddle aimed and ready to hit him. Then Mr. B. stopped and poked Manuel with the paddle and told Manuel to pull his pants down. Sissy said after that, Mr. B. took the paddle, aimed it again and hit him three hard licks. The last time, Manuel fell forward. He hurried to get his pants pulled up, and he turned around and came back inside. Sissy said Mr. Moore and Mr. B. laughed and talked for a while, then Mr. Moore stepped on his cigarette and they went back to class.

Sissy tried not to look, because she knew Manuel was crying when he came in the front door. She said Manuel slumped over his desk, laid his head down and turned his face to the wall.

By the time Sissy finished telling us about Mr. B. and how mean and bad he is, I said, "Well, I hope Mr. B. goes right down to Hell when he dies!"

I want somebody to tell Mr. Drew, our principal, all the mean things that happened. Sissy's friends can't tell on old Mr. B. since he might do the same thing to them. But someone needs to tell Mr. Drew, and I, Vonnie Clark, might be just the right person to do it.

It is the last week of school and Mr. Drew told Sissy's class that Mr. B. won't be coming back to teach at Hobbs Elementary School next year. I hope somebody told on old Mr. B. and I hope we never have a teacher so mean again in Hobbs, or in New Mexico, or in the whole United States!

My Birthday Sleepover

February 1955

Today is my 11th birthday! Momma said I could invite Connie, my best friend in the world, for a sleepover. Connie's parents go to a Pentecostal church and they are good Christians, so it's okay for me to play with her. Except nobody knows that Connie is a Sinner.

She told me a big secret and I promised not to tell on her. When her aunt and uncle visit, her uncle lays his cigarettes on the dining table then Connie sneaks a few and she takes her little brother out to the shed and teaches him how to smoke. I get scared and nervous just hearing about it, because I'm afraid smoking can send Connie to Hell, and stealing, too! So, I told her, "Connie, you probably ought to get saved before Jesus comes, because _nobody_, not even my Momma knows when that is going to be." I said if she ever wants to, she can talk to my Momma and she will help Connie get saved.

So today, right on my birthday, Connie just tuned up to cry for no reason, and said, "Vonnie, I guess I should go ahead and get saved." So, I took her to the kitchen to Momma since I didn't know what else to do, and I said, "Momma, Connie finally decided to get saved." Momma dried her hands and looked over at Connie and said, "Well Honey, we can fix that right now." We all went to Momma's bedroom and knelt down by the bed. Momma was being extra sweet to her. "Now, Connie, do you believe that Jesus is the son-a-God?" By now, Connie was really bawling, and I tiptoed to the living room and got her a Kleenex. And in a squeaky little voice Connie said, "Yes, I believe Jesus is the son-a-God." So, Momma said, "Well Honey, this next step is easy." She said she wanted Connie to tell Jesus about her sins, so Connie said, "Well, Jesus, I am a thief." Then she told the Lord that she sneaks Uncle Charlie's Camel cigarettes and takes them without asking, and she knows that stealing is a sin. Then she told the Lord that she gets matches and takes Willie, her little brother, out to the shed and shows him how to strike matches, and they have a smoke. Her nose was running bad by then and I was glad she had that Kleenex to catch it.

Well, Momma said that what Connie needs to do next is tell Jesus she is sorry and ask him to forgive her. So, Connie said, well, she really _is_ sorry, and she will try not to steal and smoke anymore. So, Momma got up and said that we were all done, that, "Connie is saved!" She said, "Now Connie's name is written in the _Lamb's Book-a-Life_ up in Heaven!" I was glad to hear that, because nothing else felt any different. So, we all got up and Momma went back to the kitchen.

But since this was interrupting my birthday, I was glad when Connie was saved and she stopped crying and wiped her eyes, because I was still waiting to find out what Momma got me for my birthday! I really, truly, want a set of lipstick in a shiny, little bag at Woolworth's, holding three colors of lipstick, red, orange and pink, but I know better than to even dream about that. So, I have asked Momma for a new baseball and bat.

I love playing baseball and I try hard to get Sissy to play with me over on the vacant lot. She plays for a few minutes and then all of a sudden without saying one word, she will put that ball down and just start walking until she gets to the corner, then she starts crossing the street and going home, and I start begging and yelling at her, "Sissy, just 10 more minutes! Please!!" She won't even look at me! My sister is like that. When she makes up her mind, she won't even talk to you! She just does exactly as she pleases.

But since today is my birthday, I'm excited to take Connie down to Woolworth's and supposably my Aunt Mindy will be there. Seeing Aunt Mindy at Woolworth's is almost a birthday present by itself! And, sure enough we caught Aunt Mindy just before she got off work at the soda fountain. I climbed up on a stool and said, "Aunt Mindy, guess what?? Today is my birthday!" "Oh, Happy Birthday, Vonnie!" she said, smiling, and she came clear around the counter and gave me a kiss! I think Aunt Mindy loves me special, so she gave me a free piece of her chocolate pie, and two forks to share with Connie. After the pie, I wanted to show Connie those shiny little bags of lipstick. One color is Pure Pink, and then Delicate Orange, and Racy Red. But since Connie is not allowed to wear lipstick either, we just passed by for a minute and went on to the jewelry counter.

At suppertime, Momma made my favorite dinner of chicken fried steak, mashed potatoes and gravy, and chocolate cake for dessert. Then she brought out my new, wooden bat and ball she had hid behind the refrigerator. That's a place I would never think to look! "Wait a minute, Vonnie, we aren't through." Momma said, and she brought out a little box, and I didn't even think about getting another present, so I pulled off the wrapping paper and looked inside, and there was the Holy Bible. Both the New and the Old Testament. It's a lot nicer and bigger than the copy of my little New Testament I carry with me to church.

When Connie had her 11th birthday, her Momma gave her a Bible, and that's *all* she got! I would have been sooo disappointed and a little bit mad if that was me, even though it is the *Holy Bible and the word-a-God!* But I don't think that's a very good birthday present, to tell you the truth. A bat and a ball is lots better. Or lipstick.

Calvary High School and Junior College

Luther, Oklahoma   November 1960
16 years old

I've been wanting to be 16 since I was 10, and now I'm 16 *and* a sophomore in high school! Mom and Dad got scared my sister and I would backslide if we went to the public high school, so they scraped together enough money—and it wasn't easy—to send us off to a good, Christian high school here in Luther, Oklahoma. But I'm just loving it! This may be as close as we come to going to college since Brother Higgins always said college will corrupt the young folks and confuse them.

It was fun packing up to come, and Momma bought Sissy and me some new clothes. We had never been to Luther, Oklahoma, but when my parents read about Calvary School being religious and all, they agreed that sending us to a Christian high school is the best guarantee that we won't backslide. Oklahoma is so much prettier than Hobbs, with flowers and lakes and trees, and I haven't seen a tumbleweed yet!

There are lots of cute boys here and they're all good Christians. Or at least, they *claim* to be good Christians. And now, I can go on as many dates as I want. But back in Hobbs, church was the only place I was allowed to go with a boy since Preacher Higgins thinks most everyone else is a sinner, and he sure doesn't want us marrying sinners! Once I invited Danny Lee Atkins to go to Faith Pentecostal with me, and he came that once but I think Preacher Higgins scared him nearly to death with all his hollering and screechin' and carrying on about Hell.

Danny ended up sitting all by himself, since I was chosen to be the piano player at Faith Pentecostal Church (*yes!*) and people are saying I am just as good as Janie Larue! But, back to Danny, since the altar call is so important, I had to sit up front and be ready to play. And then, suddenly interrupting *everything* and *everybody*, old Brother Gilaford stood right up in the middle of the sermon, shouting and speaking in tongues! And since that means that God has literally come down to our church and Brother Gilaford was "supposably" hearing straight from the Lord, everything had to stop while we just sat and waited for the interpretation of his tongues-speaking. I kept peeking over at my boyfriend, Danny, and he looked scared. I felt sorry for him. Well, speaking in tongues scares everybody, even me, and I have heard it more than two hundred times! I *never* invited him back to Faith Pentecostal. I didn't say anything to Mom and Dad about how mortified I felt about Brother Gilaford interrupting everything and speaking in tongues, since they think it's completely normal, and I don't much think so.

But now, here at Calvary High School and Junior College, I have my own roommate, Mary Martha, and she is real nice and has a twin brother Kenneth, who is pretty cute, but I'm nearly sure Mary Martha is a thief. I only say that because my favorite blouse is missing. I brought it with me, and I always wear that top at least once a week. But, if I could, and people wouldn't laugh, I would wear it every single day. It's white with tiny blue stripes and it goes with my blue culottes.

Of course, I am not allowed to wear pants, but culottes make Mom feel better since they look more like a skirt. My Mom is still really strict, and I'm pretty used to it. But even here, she is still worried about Sissy and me sinning.

That time I went home with Patty Jackson for the weekend, us girls went swimming at the Shawnee Fishing Lake. Since Christian girls are not allowed to swim with boys at our church, Patty's boyfriend and his buddies drove their car down a little ways from us so they could swim, too. That was real nice of them, and that way we wouldn't get in trouble for swimming together. And get this—we never saw them, but they sneaked back to Patty's car and stole our clothes!

Patty realized what happened, and she had some cute, terrycloth overalls in her trunk, and she handed them to me and said, "Put these on, Vonnie", since we both knew my Mom would want me to cover myself up as soon as possible before the boys saw me in a swim suit! I pulled the overalls over my wet swimming suit and the other girls covered themselves up with their towels, and we got in Patty's car and she found those lousy boys and demanded our clothes back.

But when I told Mom about those boys taking our clothes, she *yelled* at me for wearing those pants! I couldn't believe it!

I said to her, "Mom, what was I supposed to DO?"

"Well, you shouldn't have put yourself in a situation like that."

"Well, tell me this. Was I supposed to just stay in the Shawnee Fishing Lake hiding myself in a swimming suit for the rest of my whole life?"

So now, I'm trying not to tell my Mom so much because I don't like getting yelled at over something that was a lot of fun, that is, until I *told* her. And since I don't worry much about saying and doing everything perfect now, I can make my own decisions!

I was still mad at Mom and I hung up when she called us long distance. It costs money, so maybe I just saved her a few dollars.

I, myself, Vonnie Clark, have a lot of boyfriends here and since I play the piano so amazingly, the boys who plan to be preachers have their eyes on me because some of them want to travel around singing and preaching and being evangelists until they get well-known, and then they can choose a nice big church to preach and pastor and they will end up getting rich! So, they like having a pretty, talented girlfriend just to see if she would fit into their getting-rich plan.

I always figured I would probably marry a preacher, and Daddy thinks I would make a swell pastor's wife and an evangelist's wife with my great piano playing. And I figured it would keep me in church with my mind always staying on the Lord, and believe me, having a preacher husband would do that for sure. And the money would be real nice, too. But preachers are usually bossy and boring!

Last Friday night I went with David Malone, one of my boyfriends who is here from Odessa, Texas, to a big tent revival out on Will Rodgers's road. We went to hear Oral Roberts preach. It was miles from here, but David has his own car and plenty of money for gas. His Daddy is the pastor of a big church, don't cha know!

Oral Roberts is a real famous preacher and he says he plans to build a big church and college in Tulsa, but that tent revival where he was preaching was so crowded, we had to stand around at the back listening, with no place to sit down and I was wearing my highest heels! Preacher Roberts was praying for people and they were getting slain in the spirit and falling all over the place.

We had to get special permission to leave the campus to go so far, and Sister Horn, our awful dorm mother who is so mean and heartless, said if I came in even five minutes after 10:30, I would get "campused." The boys can stay out half the night and nobody even checks up on them! But if I had been late it would mean I couldn't leave and go anywhere, not even to the Dairy Queen, which is just one block away! I did get campused once before, and since I couldn't leave to go anywhere, David Malone brought my most favorite thing in the whole world up to the girls' dorm, *a hot fudge sundae from the DQ,* not once but *twice!* Every girl on the second floor turned green with envy not only because of the ice cream but because I have such a nice boyfriend!

But here's the best thing that's happened so far. Well, the hot fudge sundaes were really nice, but here at Calvary High School and Junior College, there is a special choir, The Kingdom Singers, and they travel nearly every weekend. And it's small, only fourteen singers, and guess what? I auditioned for pianist, and I got it hands down, even though I'm only sixteen. I am so excited, and all the singers, most of them I hadn't even met because they are in college and came here last year, but oh boy, they are good! So, what this means is that I have a whole lot of great, new music to play, and it's music that our choir director Dr. Shoultz has arranged. Some of it he wrote, and it is so beautiful it gives me goose bumps! Plus, we are traveling all over the United States together, sort of like evangelists do. Yes, right here, right now, and I am having so much fun!

And this is great, too. I have been getting asked to play for the morning chapel service. And since I can play either the piano or the Hammond organ, I will just play whichever one they want! I especially like the organ, and I learned to play it in Hobbs after we built our new church.

Every Wednesday we have a Foreign Missions chapel service here. Sometimes, there is a real missionary from a foreign country preaching to us. And I always start by playing *Let the Lower Lights Be Burning* on the organ because it is so dramatic. The words are about some struggling boat looking for a lighthouse, which is supposably about a Mission field, but I don't get the connection. I play it loud and everybody seems to love it and it sets a real sober mood about the heathen dying without the Lord. I am finally doing what I love, making all this sweet music everywhere I go, and luckily, I don't worry about Hell nearly as much these days!

But every Wednesday at the Missions service the Preacher talks a lot about praying to see if the Lord wants to call us to go to the "Mission field in dark Africa" or someplace, and no, I can't see doing that! Really? Be a missionary and live in a hut someplace that is hotter than Hobbs, New Mexico? No way! I would rather marry a preacher boy. I can get myself another nice top with blue stripes and a fancy jacket and wear it with my dressy blue skirt and heels, and head on out to hold revival meetings with my preacher husband. And I guess if he wants me to play the accordion and sing, well, I can do that, too!

But, lately, I've been thinking that I might get sick and tired of smiling and shaking hands, and playing and singing all the time, being so nicey-nice to all those church people, but *especially* my preacher husband. Dr. Shoultz, who loves my piano playing, says with my talent I could just ditch that idea, save some money, and go on to college.

Maybe he's right. Maybe I will.

Epilogue

Surviving the harsh, fear-based teachings of my church was not easy. We were instructed and led by preachers who considered themselves "authorities" in scripture, and wiser than any others. Many believed they heard directly from God. These teachings fostered tremendous dependency in church members, conformity and helplessness, and as a sheltered young adult, this left me completely unprepared to manage in the world.

Because of a belief in scripture to remain "separate" from the world, participation in community activities, sports, parties with school friends, football games and movies were denied. All of these experiences, however, can help to grow a young person's confidence, competence and skill in relating, and the ability to negotiate one's own life. My fear of eternal damnation was so great, that I wouldn't agree to see a movie until my mid-twenties. I felt completely unprepared for adulthood.

After high school, I did not have the encouragement or support to follow Vonnie's dream of going to college. Instead, I was married at age 17 to a boy from our church, also a teenager. Things were supposed to be perfect. I did as I was taught and abstained from sex before marriage. Girls in particular were taught to remain "pure"*. The marriage, however, was chaotic and abusive. I left after a year at six months pregnant. My parents took me in.

Fortunately, during this difficult time, I had the steady love of my parents and their compassion. My mother, a painfully honest woman, was quite vocal about her own questions and

*"How the 'extreme abstinence' of the Purity Movement Created a Sense of Shame in Evangelical Women", by Julie Ingersoll, University of North Florida.

the inconsistencies of scripture; such that other church members were uncomfortable with her candor. She spoke often about the church's practice of discrimination against women. Her value of equality for all had a great impact on me for the rest of my life.

While living with my parents, I enrolled in the local community college and worked as a secretary to support my baby and myself for the next few years. It was a time of profound confusion. I didn't know if I should or could trust my own decisions. I had no guidance or grounding for what to do or how to deal with my situation. I had followed the rules, and yet everything fell apart. Divorce, according to church teaching, would mean I was committing adultery if I remarried.

I needed compassion, not more rules and judgment from the church. As time went on, I realized nothing would change for the better if I did not set goals and take charge of my own decisions. Gradually, my dreams and goals surfaced.

I began to apply for college loans, making a plan to take my child and move to a nearby town to get an education. I needed to turn things around and join those "regular" people who worked and had fun and went to movies and football games, and to the beach in the summertime. I wanted desperately to be free of the oppressive, shaming rules of the church. I wanted to be an *ordinary person*. I questioned the way my life had always been controlled and I saw how guilt and shame and the threat of Hell had forced me to conform to rules I didn't agree with.

At 25, I met and married Ron Henry who had many of the same issues and doubts about his own church. He believed it was normal and necessary to ask questions about God, church doctrine, or anything else. Ron was relentless in his search for truth. I allowed myself the same privilege. I knew in my heart the church's teachings were severe and unreasonable. We were trying to follow archaic rules set for a different era and a vastly different culture—scriptures written in the first century and long before.

I was finally able and willing to ask these questions: If God is loving, why was there such harshness in our church doctrine? Why were good people excluded and damned? I couldn't understand why a black family member wasn't welcome to attend our church. Why was my auntie, a woman dealing with desperate family problems, condemned to Hell for smoking? Why did an upstanding community allow the beating and unbearable humiliation of a 12-year old Mexican child in the public school? Why was I sexually molested? And almost worse than anything, I could not reconcile my eight-year old cousin being taken away to live a terrible life, physically and sexually abused.

As I sat with these questions, I began recognizing that Hell is *here*, in the suffering we experience, and in the suffering we see all around us. I was in my thirties when I stopped believing in Preacher Higgin's "lake of fire", and it was a profound time of personal freedom and deliverance. For the first time in my life, I felt unafraid, authentic and finally comfortable in my own skin. I am convinced that I know where Hell *is*.

Although delayed by my circumstances, I continued my education at the University of New Orleans and the University of Kansas and received my Bachelor's degree in Music Therapy, at the University of Kansas. I worked as a Music Therapist for some time, then went on to get a Master's Degree in Social Work from the University of Kansas. I then worked with families and children in various clinical settings for over 25 years.

In my career, the scriptural Beatitudes were the guiding light in my choice of Social Work and are to the present time. I believe Social Work is God's work; *lifting up the poor and downtrodden and rectifying injustice.* These values continue to be my passion and prayer, and I will always be a proud member of the Social Work profession.

I am profoundly thankful for the talent I have, and the gift that music gives me. I still treasure playing gospel music and I play the piano almost every day. Earlier in my life, I played for and personally rubbed shoulders with some of the worst of them: famous televangelists, who preach hell and damnation, who emphasize our worthlessness and gain vast wealth from the wages of the poor.

I am grateful to all who have contributed to the richness of my life; those who have believed in me and have supported the writing of this book. I especially treasure my mentors and teachers who believe, as I do, that we are all imperfectly perfect exactly as we are.

Acknowledgments

I never had a plan to write this book, but my love of story and the encouragement of family and friends helped make it happen.

Special thanks to Joe Kellermann, who had full faith in me and the value of my storytelling. Between coffee, hikes and deep soul sharing, Debbie George assisted with edits, and encouragement to follow through and make this book happen. Jessica Castillo, very dear daughter-in-law, designed the front book cover. My children, and Ron Henry as well as my other dear friends, encouraged me and believed in the worth and importance of sharing my experiences and my truth.

Thanks also to Tracy McClellan at TQM Communications, LLC, for her assistance.

Author's Biography

Voncille Henry, MSW

BSW, University of Kansas, Music Therapy

MSW, University of Kansas, Clinical Social Work

Voncille maintained a Clinical practice for over 20 years in Mental Health Clinics, Schools and Hospitals.

www.mysinsthebook.com